ABUNDANT LIFE
1927-2013

ABUNDANT LIFE
1927-2013

CARVEL WOLFE

With parenthetical insertions by Margaret Wolfe

authorHOUSE®

AuthorHouse™ LLC
1663 Liberty Drive
Bloomington, IN 47403
www.authorhouse.com
Phone: 1-800-839-8640

Cover Design by Brian Behm

Published by AuthorHouse   12/17/2013

ISBN: 978-1-4918-4028-3 (sc)
ISBN: 978-1-4918-4029-0 (e)

Any people depicted in stock imagery provided by Thinkstock are models, and such images are being used for illustrative purposes only.
Certain stock imagery © Thinkstock.

This book is printed on acid-free paper.

CHAPTER 1

The Early Years

I, Carvel Stewart Wolfe, was born to Pearl Esther Stewart Wolfe and John Calvin Wolfe on 11 June 1927 in Minneapolis, Minnesota. Pearl was born and raised in Baltimore, Maryland, while Calvin was born and grew up in Groten, South Dakota. They met while both attended the University of Wisconsin. My dad, called Calvin, was the Colonel of the Cadet Corps at Wisconsin, and the leader of their annual military ball dance. Pearl had a major in physical education and danced in the University productions, mostly ballet.

Calvin took Pearl as a date to the military ball. While at Wisconsin, Calvin was offered an appointment to the U.S. Military Academy at West Point. However, he turned down the appointment as World War I was ending and he wished to pursue a "civilian career." Also Pearl, to whom he was engaged, didn't want a military life.

Several years after graduation, they were married in 1924 in Minneapolis where Mom taught in high school, and Dad worked as a salesman for Union Carbide. In 1930, our family of three moved to Baltimore to be with Pearl's parents, the Stewarts.

My memories of Minneapolis are few but vivid. In particular, I remember the heavy winter snow when I was about 2 1/2. Mom bundled me up in all the heavy winter paraphernalia, of course taking considerable time, and sent me out the front door. I trudged through the deep (to me) snow, directly to the back door and banged. The few minutes break for Mom were obviously too few and not appreciated.

Another clear remembrance occurred in the summer. While playing with several neighbor children, one of them picked up a grasshopper. He showed it to me and squeezed. Out came a brown goo. He promptly

1

proclaimed, "That's tobacco juice." Well, that was the extent of my biology education for a number of years.

Our first year in Baltimore I remember the long, partly circular, staircase that led up to my third floor bedroom in grandpa Stewart's house on Beaumont Ave. It was a big change when we moved to a small bungalow that my parents rented on the outskirts of town. It was there, on Melrose Ave. in July 1930 that my sister, Laurabelle, was born.

We had a happy family there in the small bungalow, even though the time was the very depth of the Great Depression. The times were not easy on Dad. He started a small business of selling large automatic coffee urns to restaurants, hotels, and such that needed many cups of coffee. The problem was that nobody was buying anything in the early 30's. He went bankrupt and was left with many urns in the basement that collected dust for years. I didn't know until I was an adult that we lived for several years on loans from Dad's older brother, Seth. Seth was an actuary in Baltimore at an insurance company and had a nice salary through the depression.

I was carefree and very active during those depression years. Several experiences stand out. I started mowing our corner lot of grass when only 6 or 7 years old. We had a push reel mower. Mowing proved to be my money maker all the way from elementary through high school.

Roller skating came easy with skates that buckled right onto your regular shoes. My favorite activity was riding the bike that I bought used for $7 when I was 7 years old. It was a full size two-wheel bike that, with my extra long legs, I could manage to just reach the pedals, not the ground. I had to make a running start to hop on the bike. That bike took me all over town, even downtown, as car traffic was very light. One negative: another kid was trying to hit me with a rope from the curb as I rode by in the street. I swerved out into the other lane, and was hit by a car. Landing on my face, I broke off a front lower tooth that is still jagged to this day. Otherwise, I got up and was fine.

Every Sunday, after Sunday School, I took the street car (electric) over to Grandpa's house for dinner with him and my Uncle Edgar and Aunt Della, both unmarried. Edgar was a brother of Grandpa Stewart, and Della was a sister who was widowed. Her son, Leroy Armstrong and his wife lived in Laurel MD where my family frequently visited. For doing some chores, like cleaning the bird baths and squirrel bowls in the yard, Grandpa gave me silver change that I collected in a gallon can. This money later bought my bike and accumulated over the years.

One winter I rode my bike to a local pond that was frozen. The activity was to run and slide on the ice on my shoes—no ice skates. There was this weak spot in the ice where I stepped through, and fell in, grabbing the edge of the ice with my hands. Wet I was, up to the neck; water depth was over my head. But I pulled out with my hands onto the ice. Since I was wet, I didn't want to rust my bike, so instead of riding it, I pushed the bike home, a mile or so away. Mom was furious that I walked!

The major family tragedy in those years was the death of my sister in January of 1936. She died of osteomylitis, a bone infection. The day of her funeral it was minus 7 degrees Fahrenheit outside. My memory is of our living room full of flowers, and Mom taking me by the hand over to the casket. Crying, she said, "Carvel, this is the last time you will see your sister." Laurabelle looked to me so calm and pretty, as ever. The loss didn't hit me until years later. Grandpa was particularly upset. He used to show off Laurabelle at his fish market by feeding her raw oysters on the half shell. I wouldn't eat them raw, then or now.

One of the ways we got though those depression years was by eating fish. Dad went to the fish market several times each week, where Grandpa handed him a package of fish. That gift of fish was our food for most of the week. Today, I still claim my good health and longevity are due to a diet of fish.

Our children games were simple in those days. A favorite was "Kick the Can," using an empty can from the kitchen. It was similar to "hide and seek." The rules of "kick the Can" were rather simple. For equipment, you needed only an empty tin can, which you could grab from your mother's garbage can. Someone is picked by the group to be "It." The empty can was placed at home base, usually a rock or pebble. Someone ran up and kicked the can as far as he could. The "It" person had to retrieve the can and bring it back to home base. This time gave everybody else in the game time to hide. "It" then had to find the others and tag them with a touch of the hand, bringing them back to home base. However, if someone snuck through, like me, and got back to the can, he kicked it hard and the poor "It" had to start all over again, as everybody else was free to hide another time. Clearly it was hard to find an "It." I think we had some devious way to choose "It." This game goes on until the participants individually tire and leave, or it gets dark, or mothers are calling the children home.

We also played a lot of soft ball right in the street, no playgrounds, or organized teams. The only equipment needed was a bat and a ball, no gloves. If an occasional car came by, we just walked over to the curb. On the 4th of July, we had real fire crackers and either threw them in the air, or lighted them under a tin can to see how high the can would blow. On Halloween, we were good at moving porch furniture from house to house. I had fun with a pea shooter that blew peas quite a distance. The trick was to ping someone's window until they came out to chase away the shooter. Everything we did was fun, but nothing was harmful. My father told me of a prank he played as a kid on Halloween. Several of the boys would completely disassemble a horse carriage, and then they would reassemble the carriage on the roof of a barn. Imagine the owner's surprise!

There were no drugs available in my environment. The only thing I saw was tobacco, and that I turned down because of the smell and cigarette smoke. Even as a small boy, I valued my lungs and running ability. The bullies in elementary school were a threat and often chased me after school. I could outrun everyone in school, and I got into the habit of running all the way home from school each day—over a mile.

Education was taken for granted. I just did whatever I was told. At age 3, in 1930, I was sent to a private kindergarten held at the near by Presbyterian church. My grandfather paid the tuition for my parents. The next year, at age 4, I went back to kindergarten again—the only grade I ever repeated! By that time I was reading all the kindergarten books, so they moved me up to first grade the next year at age 5. Apparently I pleased the first grade teacher, a Mrs. Lee, because she chose a best student to receive a free one year scholarship at the end of each year. I received the scholarship for my 2nd grade at the Presbyterian school.

Grandpa must have ended school support, because at grade 3, I started public school for the first time, having just turned 7 in 1934.

My recollection of grandma Laura Stewart, is that she was hard of hearing and used an ear trumpet. The mechanism was a long tube, one end of which fit into her ear and the other end culminated in a large bell like the front of a trumpet. She held the bell end up in front of her whenever someone spoke to her. Apparently it worked. Grandpa whose full name was Ulysses Schuyler Stewart, had an older brother, Edgar, who always lived with him. Edgar never married and was a partner in the wholesale fish business. It was Edgar's job to do all the bookkeeping and handle financial records. Grandpa, Schuyler [Skyler] was the boss, supervising the workers in the fish stall. Schuyler also bought all the fish and seafood right from the boats at the dock, just a short distance away from his stall. He had a huge walk-in refrigerator, actually a whole room, where the seafood was kept fresh. I loved to walk into that room, look around and feel the cold on a hot day. They sometimes had terrapin turtles along with barrels of shellfish. Grandpa also had his personal chauffeur, who drove them to the market and worked in the fish stall. The chauffeur lived at the two brothers' home, so he was always available.

Unfortunately, Grandma, Laura Stewart, fell down the stairs at home in 1932 and never recovered. She died in a day or so at home. I was only 5, so I don't remember her very well. After her death, a sister of the two brothers, Della, came to live with them to keep house. Della was a widow at the time, who had been living with her son, Leroy Armstrong, in Laurel, MD.

One of my favorite summer activities was swimming. While at the Presbyterian school, I went to summer camp each year on the Bush River outside of Baltimore. The school teachers owned a cabin on the river and conducted the camp. I specifically recall the summer that a distance swim was held on the river from camp to the railroad bridge, a mile down river. After swimming, using side stroke, to the bridge with many others, I alone swam back to the camp. The instructor rode beside us in a row boat. I didn't want to quit swimming!

In the summer of 1937, my age ten, we moved to a new row house in Pimlico (an area of Baltimore) to Chalgrove Ave. just two blocks from the Pimlico race track. This was my parents' first owned home, and cost about $2900. We lived there until my high school graduation. The first year, I was in 6th grade at an elementary school several blocks away. The school athletics event that spring had a softball throw that I entered. Even though I threw the softball all the way across the school field, I didn't win that event.

Summer camps after Bush River were on the Chesapeake Bay at the YMCA camp, Camp Canoy. The location of Camp Canoy was at Calvert Cliffs, where today the Baltimore nuclear electric generating plant is in operation. My collecting instinct inspired a large collection of shark teeth that had washed out of the cliffs onto the beach. They were fossilized and were millions of years old. I had teeth from tiny specks to four inches long, carefully named, labeled, and displayed in a large box. That box was saved until I arrived as a student at the University of Arizona, where I gave the collection to the school anthropology department. It is probably still there.

In July of 1938, while I was happily at Camp Canoy, the message came that grandpa Stewart had died. Someone picked me up that day and brought me back to Baltimore for the funeral. I was crushed that he had died and cried a lot, as Grandpa was so good to me. Oddly, he was rather cruel to his daughter, my mother, Pearl, as she was never included in the weekly visits, and she was disinherited. She inherited nothing but some furniture. I didn't know about all that. His business workers considered him a tyrant, also a side that I was not aware of. Every Sunday, after Grandpa's death I continued to visit the homestead on Beaumont Ave. to see Uncle Edgar and Aunt Della.

My own private business on Chalgrove Ave. was lawn cutting with a hand pushed reel mower, no power, and a hand rake to gather up the clippings. There were some dozen customers of mine who had their lawns cut, generally once a week, at a cost of 25 cents per cut. The front lawns were quite small, but steep. There were two slopes of about four feet high each, that ran down to the sidewalk. I mowed from the top of each slope, bending over to reach the mower down to the bottom of the slope. Today,

I realize that the stoop from hands to feet performed wonders for my back and arms. That exercise served me well in later years when I took up skiing.

Over many years, my bucket of change built up. One thing I bought when I started junior high at Garrison Junior High School was a new balloon tired bike for $25. It had fat tires about 3 or 4 inches in diameter, with an extremely good balance for the bike. I generally rode "no handed," which meant my hands were down at my sides, not touching the handlebars. The bike was guided around turns simply by shifting weight from side to side. I prided myself on reaching the school, several miles away, without touching the handle bar all the way. Of course, there were numerous cross streets, some with red lights. If I was caught by the light, I had to stop and grab the handlebar to start up. My trick was "anticipation." A block away, if the light was red, I slowed down until the light changed, and then sped up on green to get through.

Another trick I learned was how to compensate for the winter snows. To my memory, we had heavier snows, more frequently, back in the 30's and 40's than today. Global warming hadn't happened then. Anyway, the trick was to tie loops of rope around the rear tire, maybe a foot apart, all the way around the rear wheel. That way, I got enough pull in the snow and of course rode in the car tire tracks. That bike got me to both junior and senior high school all year long except for very heavy rains, when I took the trolley. School buses were unheard of.

One thing on my mind during the lawn cutting years was to do something for the memory of my sister. I remembered dearly what she said in the hospital while dying. Dr. Wilbur Stewart, a cousin of my mother, attended Laurabelle, and one day offered her a silver dime to cheer her up. She responded, "Where is one for Carvel?" At that time, I wasn't allowed in the hospital, but I'll never forget what that sweet angel said the day before she died!

Looking around, I saw a darling little angel carved out of pure white marble in the window of a monument shop on Park Heights Avenue. It was $75, and my bucket had that much change. I went to my parents with the money and asked for the angel to put on Laurabelle's grave. They looked and agreed, also buying a marble block for a base.

On the base stone they had carved,

"Our Darling"
"Laurabelle Wolfe"
"1930-1936"

The angel and base were placed on her grave in Loudon Park Cemetery one of those years while I was in Garrison Junior High. There is a very sad note to the story. Some years later, before I graduated from high school, the angel was found knocked off its base and smashed. I learned how low life can be lived by the vandals of our sick society. The cemetery management removed the pieces so that we would not view the tragedy. At the present time, the base with its lettering is still on the grave, but the angel has never been replaced. What should be done?

One of the groups which caught my interest as a youth was the Boy Scouts of America. I joined at the required age of 12 and passed through the ranks of tenderfoot, 2nd class, 1st class, Star and Life. By the time I got near the top rank of Eagle Scout, I was busy with high school activities and never quite finished. Age 12, in 1939, was an important year. Not only did I join the Scouts, but also that year I joined the Methodist church as a full member. Age 12 was required for adult membership.

Another big happening around that time, November 1, 1938, was the renown match between horses Seabiscuit and War Admiral. It was most unusual to have a race between only two horses instead of the normal dozen or so. It was the event of the year at Pimlico race track. Well, I didn't miss, but of course I didn't spend a quarter to get in. Only two blocks away from home, I climbed a telephone pole across the street from the track, high enough to see over the fence. I watched those 2 horses streak by in front of me, and then disappear around the turn. The finish was out of sight, so I went home to hear on the radio who had won. Seabiscuit, the underdog won in a big upset. I, along with everyone else had expected War Admiral to win. There's a whole book out on the fabled career of Seabiscuit. At the time, I didn't imagine that the race was that significant.

Another memorable event of the 30's was the New York World's Fair in 1939. It was held in Flushing, New York, just outside of New York City and lasted for two summers, '39 and '40. The Fair showed off innumerable modern or futuristic exhibits and many entertainment shows.

The ones that impressed me enough to still remember them today were the water show and the exhibits of the very latest technology. Dad drove Mom and me up to New York in mid summer. It was only a day's drive from Baltimore and we spent a long, hot day at the fair from early till late. My feet hurt till I could barely walk because I was wearing flat shoes or moccasins. What a mistake! Ever since I've worn shoes with arch support.

Well, the best show was in the pool of a huge amphitheater of some 10,000 seats—the "Aquacade." I was thrilled to see Johnny Weismuller, the olympic swimming champion, and the portrayer of Tarzan in the movies. He dove off the high dive at one end of the pool and swam to the other end. The splash was enormous! From his feet and arms as he swam, waves were running to the sides of the pool. What an eye opener! That one sprint was it for Johnny, just a few seconds in the pool. The rest of the water show consisted of synchronized swimming and all sorts of colored fountains in beautiful designs—the very latest high tech.

Another building had a ride in a moving seat that went past the latest inventions. I liked the future city with little cars running on the thoroughfares. The very latest was the clover-leaf intersection, where no car stopped in crossing a perpendicular highway. At the time I didn't think such innovation would ever come to pass!

An exhibit by GE showed the very first refrigerator and then the improved refrigerator over each year to the present (1940). The latest was a nice looking box (with one door) that actually froze ice cubes. Our boxes at home were real iceboxes with a 25-pound block of ice for the cooling. The iceman came to the back door of our house in his truck, carrying huge blocks of ice 4 feet high. He chipped off a piece the size of your house icebox. There were a lot more labor jobs in those days, like the milkman delivering milk to the door, and the knife sharpener man with his hand grindstone slung over his back walking the streets.

The other amazing invention at the fair was something called television. I walked in front of somebody with a hand held machine and, my goodness, there was my picture in front of me on some sort of box! It was over 20 years later before such an unbelievable miracle came into my home.

We need to pause and think. It will just blow your mind to look back and see all the incredible innovations that have come about in the last 100 years. Of course, computers and the internet and i-phones are the most dramatic communications of today. Try to explain those inventions to a fellow who is living in the 1930's!

Another passion I had was running. In Garrison Junior High, running the 60-yard dash, to my surprise I came in second. That was the first time when I realized somebody was faster than I. Anyway, in high school, I practiced and ran on the track team for three years. (High school buildings held only grades 10, 11, and 12, just three years' curriculum of school.) There I found that a lot of boys around Baltimore were faster than I. I was given the half mile or 880 yard run in track meets. I also liked to try the high jump and broad jump (you call it the long jump), but was not good enough to compete. My high school was Forest Park High and the F letter in green, awarded for running track, was a proud accomplishment.

In my senior year, I was only 16 and was competing with boys of 17 and 18. Anyway, some always outdid me in meets with other schools and state championships. My position turned out to be "also ran." In a final meet, just among members of the Forest Park team, I came in second in the 880. I still remember the runner who took first ahead of me. He grew up as a horse workout trainer and used to run the race horses for exercise while running on his feet. He also easily won the one mile track race.

My favorite subject in high school was mathematics. I took all they gave: algebra, trigonometry, plane and solid geometry. In those days no "Calculus" was offered. Two years of Latin was a required subject, now unheard of. My other language was Spanish for two years.

Those high school years came right through the dark times of World War II, from '41 to '44. I can see our principal now on stage in the auditorium announcing a momentous event. With classes called off and everybody seated in the auditorium, the principal said, "Listen to this word from President Roosevelt." Over the loud speaker (connected to a radio) we heard Roosevelt pronounce the start of war against the axis powers of Germany and Japan. Roosevelt's ringing voice said, "This day will live in infamy!" December 7, 1941. This procedure was repeated a number of times those three years, whenever a significant event or battle "victory" occurred. We were kept up with war events no matter what our interests were. Some students dropped out of school in order to enlist.

We also had a social life, mostly school dances. My mother tried to teach me ballroom dancing. To practice I used to go to the free open dances at the Kayhill Center on Saturday nights. They played 78 rpm records of all the great bands on a turn table. The only requirement for me to get in was to wear a necktie. We danced to Harry James, Benny Goodman, Guy Lombardo, Stan Kenton, Les Brown, Glen Miller, and others. It was a great age of both history and music.

Dramatically different from today was the school dress code. Every day to high school, I wore slacks with a dress shirt and necktie. The girls either wore dresses or a skirt and blouse. In cool weather, it was a skirt and sweater, leading to the term "sweater girl" for an attractive girl. There were no such things as "jeans." In particular, work clothes were either corduroys or overalls with a bib, neither ever worn to school. While riding my bike I wore metal clips around my pants legs at the ankle to keep them out of the bike chain. The bike, by the way, was only one speed.

Another man who had a great influence on me was Boyd Crooks. He taught at a different church than mine, but he took me under his wing. In his home, he read to me from Paul's letter to the Ephesians, Chapter 2. In particular 2:8-9 was the climax: "By grace are you saved through faith,

11

and that not by yourselves. It is a gift of God, lest any should boast." With that urging, I accepted "Salvation" by faith and have been teaching faith ever since. At the time, I was 16 years old.

I kept track of Boyd most of my life, maybe 50 years, as long as Boyd lived. He sent me a birthday card and a Bible verse every year all those years, and he said that he prayed for me every morning in his daily prayers. That is as precious as a friendship can be!

Our senior year, 1944, was a time of serious thought about the future. The boys all faced military service of some kind. The motto was "Uncle Sam Wants You." In June of 1944 the school held two formal dances at hotels in downtown Baltimore. One was the senior prom and the other was an alumna ball held right after graduation. On each occasion, I wore a rented tuxedo with the stiff white shirt and a bow tie. As was the custom, I gave each of my dates, two different girls, a white orchid corsage. The music was live, provided by one of the big bands of the day. Of course the girls wore evening gowns, all the way down to the floor. In this formal attire, we still rode the streetcar downtown and back. It didn't bother us if we had a long walk at one end.

Graduation, the second week of June 1944, was an event that stands out like no other except, probably my wedding day. That week for me was highlighted by three life changing episodes of sudden maturity. First was the graduation itself in the school auditorium, where we marched in to the tune of "Pomp and Circumstance." The honor students crossed the stage first, receiving the diploma from our principal, a man with a PhD degree. I was about fortieth out of 400 some students, enough to graduate with honors. That same week recorded my 17th birthday on 11 June, 1944. There was no big birthday party, just the frightening knowledge that I was now a "man" on my own. The Third great event of that week was my enlistment into the military service.

Since I was only 17, I was not eligible for "active" service. Instead, there were two educational programs: the Navy, V12 program, and the Army A12 program. Both programs put you under military command with military pay, but sent you to colleges for engineering training. You automatically went "active" on your 18th birthday. Well, I first applied for the Navy V 12 and was ordered to the Baltimore Fifth Regiment Armory for an extensive physical exam. We were stripped naked and thoroughly checked. Everything went fine except my eyes. I wore glasses and could not pass the eye test without the glasses. The Navy wanted 20-20 vision, so I was rejected.

I went directly to the Army, A 12, and applied all over again with all the same paperwork and physical exam. Guess what! They sent me back to the Fifth Regiment Armory for exactly the same physical. It was rather humorous since this was only several days later, and I was seeing the same doctors with all the same tests. The Army allowed glasses, so I passed and was accepted. All this happened that monumental week of my 17th birthday.

Carvel, age 1, 1928

4 Photos: Carvel & sister Laurabelle 8 & 5 years old, Carvel
& Laurabelle with uncle Edgar 1930, Carvel with Mother
& Father 1945, Carvel with neighbor friend (1935)

CHAPTER 2

The Sunday Visit to Grandpa Stewart and Uncle Edgar

Here I am recalling the very personal and highly unique experiences of travel and fun in the era of the 1930's. Today most people have never heard of or seen the conveyances of those days!

My Sunday started early with a walk over a mile to our Methodist Church in Pimlico. I attended Sunday school classes made up of all boys, taught by men. Those men made a life-long impression on me that has kept up my faith all these long years. Mr. Matthew was my teacher while I was in sixth grade, aged 10, and in Junior High. Often he just put down the lesson book to tell a Bible story by heart. Those stories solidified my faith in Jesus the Christ. Next in my life was the teacher Mr. Sisson, who not only taught but lived the life of Jesus. I've tried to be like him in my life. Finally, in the last years of my high school '43 and '44, the teacher was Bob Machin, another very devout man. O that the world today had more teachers like these.

From when I was 10 until I was 14 my spring, summer, and fall Sunday routine meant that after Sunday School I walked over to the streetcar terminal in Pimlico, just a few blocks away. There I found the car with the right number displayed on the front to take me into town, i.e. Baltimore. These streetcars were called "trolley cars," and they ran on railroad tracks. Above the car was a long springed arm that reached up to the overhead wire. A roller at the top of the arm rolled along the overhead wire picking up electricity to run the car motor. In rural areas, the car ran along the tracks at a good clip, maybe 25 miles per hour. In general a pair of tracks ran down the middle of the road so cars could go by on either side, one in a direction and the other in the opposite direction. Likewise the trolleys traveled in opposite directions on the 2 tracks.

I was always alone on the trip. My sister, Laurabelle, had died the previous year, and my mother, Grandpa's daughter, was never invited. Grandpa and my mother were estranged. I never knew why exactly, but probably he couldn't accept her marriage. From a small platform, I climbed up the steps into the trolley. I put a nickel, the 5 cent fare, into a coin slot. The nickel dropped, striking a bell to let the conductor know a fare had been paid, and continued to drop into the collection box. I think adults paid a 10 cent fare. Note the economy of the day! Upon entering the trolley car, I requested and got a transfer slip from the conductor. The paper slip had two sections, perforated between, so you could tear them apart.

In Baltimore, I got off at maybe Belvedere Avenue to catch the cross town bus. This was a regular bus, running on tires, as the street had no tracks. The bus driver took one of my transfers and crossed east to York Road. York Road ran north all the way to York, PA.

On York Road, I boarded another trolley, giving the conductor my second transfer, and rode out north towards the city limit. While still in Baltimore City, I got off at Beaumont Avenue to walk the last bit to Grandpa's house. There was, on each bus or trolley car, an overhead cord next to the window to pull to sound a bell when you wanted off the trolley. The ride in 3 conveyances took at least an hour.

Grandpa lived on Beaumont, several long blocks east on the left side. The walk was down a fairly steep hill, up the other side and then flat to the house. Grandpa's 3 storey house was on the front side of the lot, but he owned the land out back all the way through to the next street behind. That back lot was mostly covered with big trees, but grew enough grass that I had to water the grass with a hose. My chores, which I did when I first arrived, included cleaning and filling a dozen water bowls set on the ground for the wild animals around the property—mostly squirrels. I picked each one up and wiped it with my hands and carried it to the faucet and put it back again. I did that chore year-round.

Also in the back yard was the rose garden with several dozen rose bushes of many colors. All season long, Grandpa's dining room table and the tables nearby had vases of fresh roses. I watered the rose bushes each Sunday in the summer.

You entered the house across a large covered porch that ran across the front of the house and down the left side. Just inside the door was a waiting room, leading to a hall back to the dining area and kitchen in the rear. On the right was the living room and on the left was the base of the circular staircase going up to second and third floors. Behind the living room was a formal dining area that I never used. We always ate in the room next to the kitchen. A platform on the second level had the entrance to Uncle Edgar's library. Edger was the educated brother and had hundreds of books on display.

After my chores, I washed up for dinner and sat at the last seat on the side near the kitchen. At the end of the table next to me was Uncle Edgar, while Grandpa sat in the other end seat at the far side of the table. All other guests sat on the two long sides of the table. I guess the table sat 10 persons. Others at the table would be Grandpa's chauffeur, Aunt Della, and any friends or neighbors. The immediate neighbors next door were very close friends, as well as another family on Beaumont near by. Uncle Edgar almost married a lady in that family but it didn't happen. Grandpa had married, of course, but his wife was dead by this time.

I was wearing my "Sunday best" the only good clothes that I had back in the 30's. Grandpa was well dressed, but somewhat informal—just a shirt. Edgar would have on a vest, a very crisp white shirt, and some kind of hand tie. Aunt Della would bring the dishes of food out from the kitchen and line them up on the table. The meat, usually a big ham or maybe chicken, was always placed in front of Uncle Edgar. He did the carving and served each person. If the platter was filled with chicken, I always got drumsticks, my favorite. The drumstick is the lower leg of the chicken. I liked the drumstick because I could hold the small end and bite off the meaty end of the bone. Most other foods I had to tackle with knife and fork. Edgar sliced the ham and served each person. There were more than ample leftovers at each dinner. Edgar would offer and push seconds. I remember because at my house there were never leftovers—the meal was skimpy. And, although the Stewart brothers sold seafood, they didn't have fish at Sunday dinner.

The table had a formal cloth on the top that was fresh and ironed and each place had an ironed cloth napkin. Della wore a bib type fancily embroidered apron. The end of every dinner was a fancy dessert—fresh baked cake or pudding. Dinner was probably around noon up into early afternoon. All the food and dishes were cleared by Della, and she must have hand washed them—no help or machines. I wasn't expected to help, and the housemaid would be off on Sunday. I don't remember either of the brothers saying a prayer or grace for the meal. Aunt Della and I would have prayed silently.

After eating, I went right to Grandpa in the adjacent room. This routine lasted while he was living, one year, up to 1938. He gave me shiny new silver coins—a dime or a quarter—for doing my chores. I saved them all for years and had a sizeable collection in a bucket at home. Every so often at home, I would dump the bucket on the floor and line up the quarters in one place, the dimes in another, the nickels in another and count them all up and tell my mother that I had so many dollars and cents. It was this money that I eventually used to purchase an angel statuette for Laurabelle's gravesite.

In each of Grandpa's rooms was a spittoon—that is a small brass pot on the floor. Grandpa chewed tobacco and spit the excess into the pot. I didn't like it, but kept my mouth shut.

Next I would go up to the library to Uncle Edgar's room where Uncle Edgar was sitting in his huge swivel chair. He held a box of the very best most tasty chocolate candy. Of course, he was offering me several pieces. That was a real treat. I also remember that he would pull out an awesome gold watch from his vest pocket to tell me the time. It had a gold chain tying it to his vest button. Timepieces, in those days, were very expensive and not widely owned. I eyed that watch carefully.

After Grandpa's death, Edgar would be the one to give me the silver coins. I remember him best because I visited him for three years after Grandpa's death.

I had to leave the house in time to get home before the end of the afternoon. My route was an exact reversal of the trip to Grandpa's, the same trolleys, bus, and walks in the opposite direction. Near home, I got off the trolley at Chalgrove Avenue well before the Pimlico terminal. Home was just over two blocks down the street on Chalgrove. I should mention that in good weather, I actually rode my bike to Grandpa's on Sunday to avoid the long car rides. That way I saved the two nickel fares.

These visits occurred weekly over a four year period. They happened during a most memorable and maturing time for a young boy living in those years that were difficult for adults—1937 to 1941. Grandpa died in the summer of 1938, and Uncle Edgar died in 1941. They both lived into their late 60's, not like the long life spans of today. The world was suffering depression and plunging into the beginning of World War II. My recollections are of a happy, carefree and fun time with my only responsibility my education in school.

Carvel, 1944, high school graduation

CHAPTER 3

Army Life

My first assignment, starting the first of July in 1944, was the A12 unit at the University of Pennsylvania in Philadelphia. Formal classes with the civilian professors took up most of each day, but we had marching drill each day with the military officers. It was very similar to college ROTC except that we lived under military authority at all times that we were not in the academic classes. We were housed in dormitories and ate in the cafeteria. The only "free" time was in the evening when we were in our rooms, supposedly studying—at least *I* was studying.

The classroom academics were rather easy for me, at least the mathematics, as I had already learned it in high school. Apparently other high schools hadn't gotten that far in math. The physics and mechanics were more of a challenge. A college semester of work was completed in a three month period.

For the second semester, beginning in October, I was transferred to Virginia Military Institute, (VMI) in Lexington, VA. The picture in my mind of VMI is of a 3-story dormitory built in a rectangle with an open square in the middle. The center of the square located the "guard house," a sort of gazebo from which every room in the dorm was visible. Each room door faced the gazebo so someone could see any motion from the center. The surveillance didn't bother me as I was at my desk for study hours. The math was analytic geometry and calculus, both new to me. We also had military subjects like map reading and compass plotting. Every day there was a formal parade on the open parade grounds.

On weekends, we got leave or a pass to go to nearby towns. I particularly remember hitchhiking to Roanoke, VA. Hitchhiking was no problem during the war as there were always people picking up us service men. I went every where without any concern about transportation, and at no cost. In Roanoke the main activity, other than sightseeing, was the local "canteen" for servicemen. They always had refreshments and dancing with volunteer girls. On one occasion, I hitched all the way to Bristol, VA, on the border of Tennessee, which wasn't very smart. By the time I got there, it was about time to start back!

I stayed at VMI for two semesters. The fall semester ended with Christmas vacation, Christmas 1944. My Dad, Calvin, was also in the army as a lieutenant, and later as a captain. To go back a bit, he signed up while I was still in high school and at that time was in charge of an artillery battery at Fort Totten on Long Island, NY. Over Christmas vacation of my high school senior year, I visited Dad at Fort Totten. The new experience for me was learning how to drive. Dad assigned his first sergeant to teach me in the old family Plymouth. Other than backing into a tree, I guess I learned to drive ok. Those lessons from the sergeant were the only lessons I ever had. I didn't get a driver's license until many years later in Tucson, at the U. of Arizona.

Anyway, by Christmas '44, Dad was teaching the ROTC at Texas A and M University and had a small cottage next to campus, in which he was living with Mom. They had sold the Baltimore house near Pimlico racetrack and had moved to Texas. My Christmas break between semesters at VMI was mostly a train ride to Texas.

The most memorable unique experience of the time happened after visiting my parents in Texas. On the train on the way back to Virginia, an MP (Military Police) asked me to show my leave papers. The "papers" had accidentally been left on my desk back at VMI. Well, I could have been arrested on the spot and hauled off the train. It took some mighty fast-talking on my part to convince the MP to let me go and return to VMI.

The next semester at VMI ended the last of March 1945. Almost all of my group, who had now reached 18 years, were sent to active duty. Very few in the A12 program got to a fourth semester. However there was a 4th semester offered at none other than Texas A&M where my parents were. That was a very happy experience, spending the last classes of my engineering program near my parents' new home. I particularly remember a course in surveying. We surveyed the campus and drew a topological map—a lot of fun. Another course in Electrical Engineering seemed very difficult, so that I mentally decided not to major in engineering.

My full year in the A12 program ended the last of June, followed by several weeks off at home in July. Next I was ordered to a replacement depot near San Antonio for active duty assignment. Of course, August 1945 was the end of the big war with the atomic bombings at Nagasaki and Hiroshima. The result was that I got credited with one month of active duty before the actual signing of the peace treaty with Japan, which ended the big war. So officially, that made me a World War II veteran.

While at the depot in San Antonio, and on guard duty, I stood near a spot where an officer was disciplining some AWOL (Absent Without Leave) men. The officer went through all of the procedures used by military and civilian authorities to track down those who were trying to run away. That lecture proved to be a most fortunate experience, as I was asked later at Camp Roberts to speak on the same subject before a panel of officers. They were interviewing me as a possible officer candidate. I gave the panel the same speech over again, practically word for word, as I had heard it a number of times.

Near the end of August 1945, I was shipped (by train) to Camp Roberts, California for my 17 weeks of basic training. That was the full combat training before an overseas assignment. Mine was the last group to go through the full 17 weeks, including baptism by live fire. We concluded combat training by crossing a field on our stomachs with live fire whistling overhead. The very next group in Camp Roberts had a shortened basic of about 13 weeks, with the live fire eliminated. Right after the war ended, the Army stopped the live fire in training since someone always got hit because of carelessness.

The 17 weeks of basic training were rather routine and arduous. My track experience in high school was a bonanza, since I could run any distance. One-mile runs in training were a breeze.

The weekend passes were my big joy. We could hitchhike up to San Francisco or down to Los Angeles, as Camp Roberts was about half way in between. One weekend in San Francisco, at a local canteen, they were featuring talent from the attending servicemen. One large man got a call to sing. He sang "Old Man River" with a very deep baritone voice. He had a voice as good as any professional, and maybe he was formerly a pro. Anyway, he was the best I ever heard, and the singing brought tears to my eyes.

One weekend in Los Angeles, I attended a church in Hollywood, not far from my favorite canteen. That was the famous Hollywood Canteen, where real pro movie stars came in to dance with the servicemen. Goodness knows who I danced with. They could have been any of the current celebrities. Anyway, seated in the Hollywood church, 'way back in the sanctuary and up in the balcony, I enjoyed the service. As I was walking out, a strange woman stopped me and invited me to dinner at her house. She was elderly and most sweet. Of course, I went and consumed a terrific meal at her nearby house. She may have been living alone. After the food, as I was about to leave, she asked me to take along a poem, a memento from her. I memorized that poem and have carried it in my heart ever since. The thought has helped and encouraged me over all these years. I share the poem with you:

> It is my joy in life to find
> At every turning of the road,
> The strong arm of a comrade kind
> To help me onward with my load.
> Since I have no gold to give,
> And only love can make amends,
> Be this my prayer whilst I shall live:
> God, make me worthy of my friends.

My basic training concluded in December of 1945, after WWII had officially ended. During my final simulated battle at Camp Roberts, there were two outstanding experiences. With the others in my squad, we crossed a deep ravine on a rope with a second rope overhead to hold on to. Explosives were being set off in the earth below. As I neared the far side, my steel helmet somehow came loose and fell off, rolling down into the ravine. I hurried off at the end of the rope, and immediately ran down the slope to recover the helmet. On the way back up, I remembered the explosives and the fact that I could have been caught. Maybe someone was watching, who knows.

The second experience was also dangerous. Our "battle" was nearing conclusion as I and several others were climbing a hill to "take out" a machine gun nest on the top of the hill. We charged into the machine gun position and I grabbed the hot barrel of the gun, fortunately with leather gloves on, while a buddy held the other base end. We carried the 50-caliber gun all the way down the hill to a service road below, where our pick up was at the end of the battle. I was so proud of the capture that I thought I would get a commendation. Well, of course we never heard anything!

Before leaving Camp Roberts, I was told by the commander that I had been chosen for OCS—Officer Candidate School. Part of the reason for my OCS choice was undoubtedly the stellar talk I gave to the reviewers on the subject of AWOL. It's just amazing how the details of your life work out for the good. He told me I could take training for a 2nd lieutenant, provided I signed on for several more years of military service. However, I turned down the invitation because the war was over.

The war ended in August, after our first month at Camp Roberts. There were maybe 10 million men up for discharge at the end of the war. A point system was inaugurated, which allotted so many points for each month of war service. The total number of points determined the order of discharge. I had only one month time in before the end of the war, so consequently, the lowest number of points. My prospects were that I would serve over a year in the army before a discharge.

However, there was an alternative to just continuing service while waiting, possibly several years, for a discharge under the point system. The army offered a special one-year enlistment, just for waiting men until they could be processed out. If I signed on, I knew that I would be discharged at the end of the year's enlistment. It was most likely the fastest way out, so that was my choice instead of OCS or other options. My goal was to get back to college for more education.

From Camp Roberts, I was sent to Fort Ord in northern California. There, I re-enlisted for a year. That re-enlistment gave me some weeks of leave, plus travel money to any desired location for the next assignment. I chose Maryland to get the most time, plus the most money. After visiting my parents, I continued across the country to Fort George Meade in Maryland. All travel was by train in those days.

At Fort Meade, I was chosen to serve my overseas year in Panama, in the U.S. Canal Zone. It's interesting that the government was still trying to protect the famous Canal after the war. To me it was a most fortunate and delightful assignment.

After a train ride from Fort Meade that circled all around the U.S. eastern country side, a security measure, we got off in New Orleans for shipping. My ship was an old converted Liberty Ship called Cape Mears. The cargo hull was filled with hammocks for the troops. Imagine the air and stench with hammocks hung over top of one another down in an unventilated enclosed hull as you head into the hot tropics. I never slept in my hammock. At night I crawled up onto a tarpaulin stretched across the stern of the ship to offer shade below. In the morning, I was awakened by a "billy" club poking me from below. The club belonged to an MP (Military Police) who ordered me down. The policeman explained that I was off limits and in danger of rolling off the tarp directly into the ocean! Ah, the wonders of youth! Of course, we landed on the Atlantic side of the Canal and then took the railway across to reach the Pacific side. I still see the Panamanian boy running up to the train window to hand me a whole bunch of bananas in exchange for a dime. They were good eating!

I was stationed at a small post called "Corrizal" that housed the local signal corps units. They ran and maintained the area radio facilities for communication. I personally worked with a civilian who was an expert repairman for the towers and large substations. We traveled around from towers on top of a mountain to units hidden underground. My work was just handyman for the civilian.

Our post was just a short, easy bus ride from Panama City, on the south, or Pacific Ocean side of the canal. The Caribbean Sea, or Atlantic Ocean, is on the north side of the Canal Zone. The Canal Zone was a

10-mile wide strip across the Isthmus of Panama—5 miles on each side of the canal itself. The U.S. maintained this strip to protect the canal which otherwise would be in Panama. It was important for Naval ships to travel without fear of sabotage. The canal runs north to south because of a bend in the land strip between the two Americas. The railroad ran across the Canal Zone from the port Colon in the north to Panama City.

I more or less worked a 5-day week and had weekends off. The weekends became eye-opening travel sights. Of course, Panama City was a frequent destination. Most impressive was the church of the golden altar. The whole front of the church, from floor to ceiling and side wall to side wall, was decorated with elaborate carvings completely covered with gold leaf. An enormous amount of gold was used, and the only reason the gold was not taken by the Spanish or others was that it was painted white to look like ordinary wood. Only in recent times had the paint been washed off to reveal the pure gold.

Another outstanding trip was a boat ride to an island in Gatun Lake, a lake in the center of Panama. The canal uses Gatun Lake for most of the crossing of the isthmus. This uninhabited island was pure virgin rain forest, not touched by man except for our walking tour. Our guide was a naturalist who helped the rare sights come alive. We admired huge ants, flying butterflies, monkeys, orchids, and a large number of wild flowers, ferns, and plants. I was so impressed—my first time in a jungle!

On another occasion I took a fishing boat out into Panama Bay and caught a beautiful large fish, probably a Spanish mackerel.

As a part of my job, I was taken out to an island in the Pacific beyond Panama Bay to work on a communication relay station on the island. The biggest job I recall was playing ping-pong with the local post members. Coming home from that island turned out to be a dramatic experience on the sea. On a rather small boat, quite old, I was sleeping on the bow deck. Suddenly, there was a jolting smash that almost stopped our boat. I crawled back aft to see what was going on. The boat captain was using our extinguisher to put the engine fire out. We could have been lost at sea. The blessing came that the fire was out and the engine still worked. Well, the Captain explained the event. The boat hit a manta ray fish. The ray could have been as big as the boat. They weigh tons. The sudden shock threw the battery cable off and started the engine fire in the old oil over the engine. We got back to port safely, to everyone's great relief. Well, that is my story of "the fish that set the boat on fire!"

In the meantime, my father, Captain Wolfe, was shipped overseas to the island of Okinawa at the end of the fighting. On the island, he commanded an army company that was there just to maintain peace. Of course, Mom was left alone at home. She decided to fly to Panama to visit me!

I spoke to the minister of a civilian church near post Corizal, where I attended the Sunday services. The minister said, "Sure, invite your Mom to stay here at the parsonage. There is an extra room." The parsonage was a nice home right next to the church. So, Mom came and lived at the parsonage for a number of months. Try to top this: How many servicemen on active duty overseas had their Mom with them, practically next door?

It was all fun and adventure for me. Every weekend, Mom and I went out on some excursion to see something. We traveled, mostly by bus, all over the countryside to see historic places. Some of the locations were old Spanish forts, Indian ruins, quaint towns, plantations, the Canal locks, and any number of colorful bazaars, or shops. Consider all this going on while I was still rank private, with no privileges.

Mom had an eye popper at the parsonage. She looked out of her second floor window and saw a native iguana 4 or 5 feet long on a tree limb just outside of her window. Actually, the iguana is harmless, but it looks ferocious, like a dragon. I believe the iguana stayed in the tree for several days. I got plenty of comment, and couldn't help but laugh.

Eventually, Mom returned home, and I finished my tour in Panama February 1947. It sure helped that I had taken two years of Spanish language in high school. You never know when something from the past will be most useful later on.

Naturally, I shipped out of the port of Colon and to the port at New Orleans. While my discharge papers were being prepared, the 1947 February Mardi Gras occurred. Of course, all my free time was spent in down town New Orleans. I watched the elaborate floats and costumes, along with band music, go by on the main thoroughfare. The Latin Quarter, streets and clubs, was overflowing with people. Music blared out of each doorway. What a happy and noisy celebration! Mardi Gras is a terrific destination for everyone at least once in a lifetime!

Carvel, 1947, discharge from army

CHAPTER 4

Beginning of Civilian Life

After collecting all my discharge papers, I took a train back to Baltimore, MD. In Baltimore, I immediately went to the downtown YMCA and rented a room. That was my home until mid-summer 1947. They had a swimming pool, ping-pong tables, and various activities. The rooms weren't private. I had an assigned roommate.

To help pay my way, I contacted my old high school, Forest Park. They immediately hired me as a substitute teacher. I filled in several times a week in a couple of subjects, but mostly math. It was no trouble for me to take over the lecture in any mathematics course, all familiar. Actually, I had just graduated from Forest Park two and a half years before and was only 19 years old. People could barely distinguish me from a student.

While I was in Baltimore, my father came home and was discharged from the army. Mom always wanted to go to Arizona for the dry climate. So the two of them started off driving west. In New Mexico, Dad checked out a position in some military college, but was told he needed a master's degree. They kept going west to Tucson in southern Arizona. Mom said, "This is it."

They bought a small two-bedroom adobe house on the north side of town, facing the Catalina Mountains. It was 2834 E. Florence Drive. At that time there was practically nothing but open desert between their house and the mountains. Now that desert is full of houses several miles out, and expensive developments right up the sides of the mountains.

Summer of 1947 saw me out of work and running out of money. I did have some social life by attending weekend dances at the girl's YWCA. Since my parents were now in Tucson and the University of Arizona was in Tucson, it was easy for me to choose the U. of A. I went home to my parents in Tucson and applied for entrance into the university. The registrar gave me college credit for my 4 terms in the A12 programs. Thus, I already had advanced standing and was accepted as a student.

The good news was Uncle Sam's college program for all former U.S. service personnel. It was called the G.I. Bill. The government paid not only my tuition and a book allowance, but also a small stipend to live on. Since I was living at home, the stipend was ample for fun and social life. A portion of my monthly check went to my parents for food. I really feel quite indebted to our government for taking care of my education from 1947 through 1951, including two degrees. Think what that would cost today—a fortune!

I really enjoyed my years at the U. of A. It is a fond memory of college life, as I look back. Social life was primarily through the fraternity and sorority system. I joined the Lambda Chi Alpha fraternity. At all of the dances and dinners, I turned down all alcoholic beverages. Actually, there were three of us "teetotalers" in the chapter, a minority, but some company. Of course, the university had school dances and class dances for all students. There were approximately 5,000 students during my years. Now the university has around 30,000 to 40,000 students. You can guess that I became a good dancer.

Perhaps more important was the academic curriculum. Since I decided to major in mathematics, I took practically all the math courses. In my third year, 1949-1950, as a senior, I already had enough credits to graduate because of the A-12 program. So I took advanced math courses for graduate credit. My bachelor degree, BS, was completed in January 1950, but my graduation was not until the once-a-year time in June 1950. The graduation was not memorable because of the mass of students. The degree was proclaimed from the podium, and the diplomas were just passed out at our seats in the school stadium. It was nothing like the individual being called and going across the stage and being personally handed the diploma by the principal. That's how I fondly remember high school graduation. Still going to school full time that fall, I completed the master's (MS) degree in January of 1951.

My parents' house was several miles from the university, so one of my first purchases was a motor scooter. That was transportation for the three years. A must see sight outside of Tucson was Mount Lemon in the Catalina mountains, some 9500 feet high. It was an easy drive to the top in a car, but my scooter had to be pedaled with one foot on the ground for the last mile. So much for the low-powered scooter! I believe, after a trip or two up Mt. Lemon, I had to have the scooter motor reconditioned.

Another trip or destination, on the way to Mt. Lemon, was Sabino Canyon, which had a small lake (extremely rare in the desert) fed by water coming down the mountain. We had both individual and fraternity picnics in Sabino Canyon. The entire desert area all along the way out of town was covered with cactus, huge saguaro, 25 feet tall, round barrel cactus, prickly pear, and many more. The desert charm is unbelievable until you experience it, especially when the cacti are in bloom. The beauty takes your breath away with all the many colored flowers along with the multicolored rocks.

Note the definition of a river in the Tucson desert: It is where all the ripples and lines in the sand go in one direction. For example, the Tucson River, going through town. It is recognized by that pattern in the sand. Perhaps once or several times a year, when there is an extremely heavy rainfall, with a huge run off down the Catalinas, water actually raged through town. On those special days, it was a thrill to go out Campbell Road to the river edge and watch the torrent. Anything loose, such as a person or car, would be swept away! Just a couple of days later, the river would be dry!

My father was a hunter, loved to go out in the hills and hike for miles. Occasionally, he came home with a javalina [pronounced HAV-a-leen-a] which is a wild pig, or wild deer for venison. He would butcher out the meat and cure the hide. During dove season he did really well and we ate a lot of dove breasts. I still have and wear two belts that Dad made for me from rattlesnakes. He shot the snake, skinned it, cured the skin in brine, and hand mounted the impressive skin on a leather background. Today it is illegal to shoot or kill a rattlesnake, so my belts are irreplaceable! Dad also enjoyed golf. He tried to teach golf to me, but the results were poor.

Both my parents liked square dancing and took me sometimes. That caught on, and I still square dance today. Margaret, my wife, and I dance regularly in several square dance clubs.

Dad and I did a lot of work on the desert around our house to convert it into an oasis. We put in a grapefruit tree and a lemon tree out back, and also a line of oleander bushes across the rear property line. We had a grape vine that grew up a trellis into an arbor, and also over the carport roof. Out front, Dad put in a blue spruce. Eventually it became enormous, maybe 40 feet high with limbs that covered the porch roof and covered the paved walk from the road up to the front porch. We had to cut out of the tree a space to walk to the front door. Across from the spruce on the left side of the yard, Dad planted low flowers to border the grass. On the far left, next to the driveway to the carport out back, we planted a cactus bed. We brought in and planted many varieties of cacti from the desert out of town. There were several barrel cacti with different color blossoms, a saguaro [so-WAR-o] with white blooms, some prickly pear, and various other smaller samples. All bloomed in the spring, making a striking display.

That saguaro, in 20 of the 30 years my parents lived there, grew to maybe 8 or 9 feet high. It was quite healthy and grew faster than it would have in the wild because it received more water in the garden. One day Dad noticed that a bird had pecked a hole in it near the crown to build a nest. He had read in the newspaper that these bird nests brought a disease to the cacti in the desert, and many of the giant saguaros out in the desert had died, so he wanted the bird to go away. He climbed a ladder, removed nesting material, and filled the hole with cement, and painted the cement green to match. Later, he saw the bird return, and puzzled, proceed to make a new hole next to the old one. Dad and the bird repeated this procedure, with holes filled all around the top of the cactus until the cactus was girdled. Unfortunately that lovely specimen died.

On a revisit to the old homestead in the summer of 2003, I saw the grapefruit tree still produced and the oleanders still bloomed almost 60 years later. My parents continued to live there in Tucson until 1980. The last year or two of their lives, they sold the property and moved into a retirement home. Mom, Pearl, died from a recurrence of cancer in May

1980. Otherwise she was in good health, and had already bought her plane tickets back east to attend the wedding of my oldest daughter, Cindy, in June 1980. Mom always told me she didn't want to be a widow and wished to die first. Well, her wish was almost fulfilled, since Dad, Calvin, died in September 1979. Their deaths were only six months apart. Dad succumbed to a stroke. Both were cremated and their urns were buried in Tucson Memorial Park, 5401 South Park Ave., Tucson. Arizona. The name, we found out when we visited in 1006, has changed to South Lawn Mortuary.

Summers at U. of Arizona

There were several enriching summer experiences during those years at the U. Of Arizona. One summer I went with a group to a sort of work camp to the inland port of Stockton, California. There we joined groups of potential day laborers at a town square where the bosses would come, pick a suitable number of workers and haul them off in a truck to the job. The jobs were greatly varied and the men were paid by the hour in cash at the end of each day. A number of days I got picked as a longshoreman, because of my healthy size. We worked either in a warehouse or down in the hold of a freighter ship loading the cargo, such as grain, canned goods, or bales of cotton. I remember being down in the bowels of a ship, carrying 100 pound sacks of wheat grain from a sling on a hoist that lowered them from dock to deck. I, by myself, then carried a 100 pound sack from the sling over to a row and stacked it up to ear high, for either an 8 or a 10 hour day. If the ship was near full, workers were not allowed to stop until the job was done!

You were paid the going hourly rate, which varied by job and selection. I don't recall just what a longshoreman was paid, probably about $2 an hour. I do remember that one day I received 10 cents an hour more than others as I had been picked as foreman. News to me!

Other jobs included field work on the surrounding farms. One day I worked in an onion field, picking up the plowed onions, cutting off the stems and placing them in a half bushel basket. We were paid by the basket. At the end of the day, the supervisor paid me in silver dollars. That must have been to impress the Mexican laborers. Of course, I saved my money, beyond minimal expenses, and brought it home.

Another summer, I joined in with a Wesley Foundation Caravan to the states of Oregon and Washington. A caravan was a group of students from a college Wesley Fellowship that went out to inspire the local youth groups at churches along our journey. My caravan had students from a number of colleges around the country. Our leader was the staff director of Wesley Foundation at our U. of Arizona. We held inspirational services at each local church, witnessing and sharing our experiences. It was a time of significant spiritual growth.

The woman leader, a single, school teacher, kept in touch with me until about 2000. She took extensive trips each summer and wrote each Christmas pages of detail about her trips.

Another summer, a carload of us from Wesley drove to the quadrennial celebration of our national fellowship at the U. of Indiana, Bloomington, Indiana. That was a weeklong program with many gatherings and workshops. The cross country drive was a first for me. We each took turns driving our director's car for several hours apiece, driving straight through, Tucson to Bloomington. This was my first on-the-road driving experience. That was when I really learned to drive!

The big event for me in Bloomington was the final massed service, several thousand students in attendance at the huge auditorium. Three of us were chosen to read the scriptural program in unison, a high voice (tenor), my voice in the middle, and a low (bass) voice. That was my first time to stand before a huge audience and perform.

Back in Tucson, for a year or more, I accepted the challenge of teaching at a downtown Chinese Methodist church. The church was mostly composed of Chinese businessmen and their families. Their services were held on Sunday afternoon and in the Chinese language. I taught the high school youth group, all boys, and in English. The boys were of course bilingual. The Sunday School class met the hour before the church service. My boys would sometimes read the scripture, at their church service, in Chinese. I was so proud of those boys, all top notch students and fully attentive. At the end of the year two of my boys were valedictorians in their separate high school graduations. When I married, four years later, four years after leaving, they sent me and Margaret a carved wooden box, which I still cherish.

CHAPTER 5

Finishing Education

The spring semester of 1951, I transferred to U. of California at Berkley, since I had gone as far as possible at the U. of Arizona. For travel, I bought a little 1940 Ford coupe for $150, and sold the motor scooter. In Berkley, I found a room in a private home very close to campus. Realizing that a Ph.D. degree was very important to teach math on the college level, I decided to go all the way. My G.I. Bill had run out, so I worked at the Berkley atomic research lab part time. My job was to grind numbers through a desk top electric calculator for some experiment in nuclear energy. Note, there were no computers in those days. I took advanced math courses at the University and certainly was busy.

In June of 1951, I didn't even bother going to the graduation for my master's degree from U. of A. By that time, I was busy looking forward to more graduate school at the University of Washington, working toward the Ph.D. degree, and besides I was employed at the Berkeley California Nuclear Lab for the summer.

Berkeley was extremely important for me, as that is where I met Margaret. As was my habit all my life, both in and out of military service, I attended church for worship every Sunday. At the Berkeley Methodist church, I also went to youth fellowship on Sunday evening. There at the youth meeting, I noticed right off a very attractive, small (compared to my 6'1" height) blonde girl. Her name was Margaret Owens and she was just visiting California for that year. Her father, Dr. Owens, had accepted a visiting professorship at the University, so Margaret spent her freshman year there. The family rented a house in Berkley Hills (mountains, actually). Their regular home was in Arlington, VA, and Dr. Owens taught at the George Washington U. in Washington, D.C.

I asked Margaret for a date, and took her out on a couple of weekends in my two-seat Ford coupe. Do I remember the hill she lived on! It was famous for testing the motor power of a car. People contemplating buying a used car would attempt to drive up that hill, and many a car was abandoned in someone's yard. My little coupe wouldn't make it to the top. After all, it was a gravity feed for the gas! I think I backed the car up part way. Anyway, half way up, I parked the car into the curb to hold it. If you were going forward, downhill, you looked right into San Francisco Bay—only the water, a mile away, visible. The flat cross streets vanished in the perspective. Those were some experiences, getting Margaret to and from her home.

At the end of the summer semester, I knew Margaret well enough to get and write down her Arlington, Virginia address in my little black book. She and her family, of course, returned home to Arlington.

[The above is how Carvel remembers it. I remember going to the movies with him a couple of times—the story of Delilah and Samson was one I am sure we saw. He would only talk about weight lifting. I was not impressed. Anyway in July, I guess, he said, incredibly, "I won't be able to take you out again because I'm going to Washington." Did anyone ever give an explanation like that! Did I care? Was I supposed to care? However in the spirit of things, I responded, "Oh, I'm going to Washington, too." It took a while for us to sort out that he meant Washington State, and I meant Washington, D.C. I always told young people in California that I was from Washington, rather than Arlington, Virginia, because their idea of eastern U.S. geography was rather hazy— even non-existent. I assumed some teacher in school had told them about the capital of the U.S. Anyway, having gone this far with explanations, I agreed to give Carvel my address. I then forgot the entire episode. And he never wrote or contacted me, and I really would have been surprised if he had. He was, to me, just an evening at the movies. Margaret]

I stayed in Berkeley over the summer of 1951, continuing to work at the lab and finding out their experiment wasn't going well. The numbers produced by all that computation did not agree with their theory. So much for computation—or perhaps their theory. Near the end of the summer, I sold off the Ford coupe for $75, and bought a 1946 Ford sedan. The 4-door cost about $400.

I wasn't too happy with the situation at U. of California. Besides, I needed financial support and free tuition. I found both at the U. of Washington in Seattle, by nailing down a graduate teaching assistantship. At the U. of Washington, I taught one freshman course while taking several, maybe three, graduate courses. The stipend was small, but they gave me free tuition. The idea was to finish all course work in two years. Of course, an original thesis was also required for a Ph.D.

Well, I stayed there in Seattle for two academic years, coming back to Tucson for part of the summer. It was a pleasant two years, especially if you liked rain. One year it started raining at Christmas and the next day without rain was somewhere in February!

I located a room in a private home just a little over a block from campus. Across the same street and a block toward the campus was the fraternity house of Lambda Chi Alpha—most convenient. I ate all my meals at the Frat house, except a Sunday dinner when the house kitchen was closed. Breakfast and lunch were informal, but dinner required a coat and tie every day. Memorable was one dinner when they served horse meat. Actually, I wore dress clothes with a tie to every freshman class that I taught.

Of course, I walked everywhere during the school year, and my car stayed parked on the street. However, that 4-door Ford was a big help with the extra room inside to transport my suitcases and various paraphernalia. I made the round trip, Tucson to Seattle, each year, coming home in the summers of 1952 and 1953.

Most of my time was spent studying in my room. There was, however, an active social life at the fraternity. I usually went to the weekend dances or parties. As usual I drank Coke. Over the two years in Seattle, I dated two different girls on my occasions. My life was too busy to think of Margaret back east. She was attending the College of William and Mary for her sophomore and junior years. [I think he only knew I was at the college when he re-connected with me later.]

I got myself a locker at the University gymnasium and made a habit of working out. Three days a week, MWF, in the afternoon after classes, I worked out in the weight room. I practiced all the standard lifts with a bar bell and adjustable weights. I knew what to do and how much weight to use from several years of practice back at U. of Arizona. My favorite lift was the "snatch." You crouched over the barbell on the floor, and then in one continuous motion brought the bar straight up over your head while squatting as underneath the bar. You than straightened your legs out straight to a full stand with the weight high over head. A "good" snatch was to lift your body weight. It took a lot of practice, but I did well. While my body weight was only 155 pounds, I snatched 160 pounds. Very few people could go over their body weight. Of course the professionals do much more. Sixty years later, I still have a strong back and shoulders from all that exercise. [A bit of spousal disagreement over that last statement. Why did he have to have a back operation? Margaret] Regardless of my disc repair operation in 1999, I still have a strong back. (Carvel) Also, sixty years later, my weight has stayed in the low one sixties, about 164.

I attended all the school games, both football and basketball. Most memorable were the basketball games. U. Of Washington had a championship team those years. The star player was "Hooks" Hubregs. He stood about 6'7" tall and had an amazing hook shot. By bringing the ball up behind his head with his right hand and then lifting it entirely over the defense man's outstretched arms, he had a clear path to the basket. It was unstoppable, and he by himself could outscore the opposing team. Of course, his teammates also made many baskets. Their team went to the NCAA final and only lost to Kansas because Hooks was fouled out in the second half.

The University of Arizona had also had a most unusual basketball season during my years there. They never lost a home game. I attended all the home games my 4 years as a student and never saw a game lost! They did lose road games and were not national champions, but always played well enough above their heads to win at home. I remember a particular game against Long Island when Long Island WAS the national champion, and Arizona won on a last second basket.

CHAPTER 6

Continuing to Teach

Near the end of my second year at U. of Washington, the mathematics chairman called me in to state that he didn't think I was able or ready to create a thesis of new material. You were expected to come up with new ideas in your field.

Anyway, that ended my employment and stay at U. of Washington. So, I started to look for another job. A teaching job came to my attention at Shepherd College in Shepherdstown, West Virginia. I interviewed with the college president in Chicago, and flew back to Seattle. The teaching position was offered and accepted before my year ended at U. of Washington.

Once again, I drove home to Tucson for the summer. By the way, that 1946 Ford gave out and wouldn't move. I think the clutch was frozen. Anyway, I gave up and traded for a 1950 Studebaker, for maybe $1100. I called it a green grasshopper. It had a pointed nose, as the engine cover was cone shaped, very distinctive, and the outside painted all bright green. Studebaker wanted you to be reminded of the aerodynamics of an airplane, since they made airplane engines. I drove that grasshopper all the way across the country: Seattle to Tucson, to Shepherdstown.

At Shepherd College, the year of 1953 to 1954, I was the entire mathematics department. I not only taught all of the mathematics courses, but also one of the physics courses. Their mathematics only went as far as a year of calculus in the senior year. Today calculus is a beginning freshman course. It was a good experience teaching all their courses: algebra, trigonometry, analytic geometry, and calculus.

Guess what! I looked into my little black book and found Margaret's address in Arlington, VA. I wrote her a letter and she invited me to Thanksgiving dinner at her home. It was an easy drive from Shepherdstown to Arlington. In Arlington, it was very pleasant to meet her family and see Margaret again, with a good home-cooked meal.

I had interesting chats with Dr. Owens, Margaret's father. He was interested in how I could explain more than 4 dimensions or 4 dimensional space. With momentum and electron spin, I got up to 8 dimensions, so he was impressed. Of course in abstract mathematics, we even work with infinite dimensional space. The number of dimensions is just a change in the formulas representing that space. You don't need to visualize the space and you can work formulas in any dimensional space.

That Thanksgiving led to a number of visits down south. By the spring semester of 1954, I was driving all the way to Williamsburg, Virginia to visit Margaret on special occasions over weekends. We went to her sorority parties (Gamma Phi Beta) and school dances. Margaret notes: [In the fall, after driving home Sunday night in poor conditions, he wrote me that he couldn't come often because of the need to be at Shepherdstown early on Mondays. The next thing I knew, he had rearranged his teaching schedule for the spring so that he had no Monday classes. Remember he was the entire math department. He gave himself long weekends so he could drive often to Williamsburg.]

Margaret graduated May 1954, and I finished my year at Shepherdstown. For Margaret's graduation, I was there and helped move all her stuff from her sorority room back to her home in Arlington. [Margaret adds: I shared my Gamma Phi Beta dorm room with Mary Anderson, who was a smoker and a constant coffee drinker, and as untidy as they come. When Carvel walked into the room to carry stuff out, he saw coffee cups, hers, that had sat around so long they had grown mold— did you know that could happen? The room was a total disaster. He later commented that he should have realized that housekeeping wasn't my forte. But I have learned since. People do change.]

Summer 1954, I found a job in Washington at the Department of Commerce in the World Tide Computation Department. They had a mechanical machine with little pulleys to represent the sine waves of the forces of the moon along with all the other forces acting on local tide water

41

for each area of interest. I had to hand crank the machine. Once all the amplitudes were set on the machine, it progressively added all the forces and showed the times of high and low tide for each day of the year. I had to be sure to stop cranking at the right moment. We then had to check the results for consistency and send them to the printer of the tide tables. It was mostly routine work. By the way, that machine is now a relic stashed in the Smithsonian Museum. Now, all computation is done by computer.

However, there was time for fun. One of the department pros challenged me to derive a formula for the derivative of the function of X to the X power using the binomial theorem. I wrote out and handed him the derivation. He was quite impressed and unhappy that I left after 3 months, June, July, and August. He wanted to keep me. I left to accept a teaching assistantship at the University of Maryland at College Park.

That summer started the rest of our lives together. In June I asked Margaret to marry me. I drove around with her one evening looking for a good place to propose, and led her into the vacant sanctuary of Community Methodist Church, her home church, to ask her. She accepted and set the Thanksgiving holiday weekend for the wedding date. That made the date a Wednesday, November 24 of 1954, after classes at U. of Maryland.

Margaret obtained a scholarship at the University of Maryland to pursue her master's degree in English, starting in September. It paid full tuition plus $75 a month, an amount calculated to pay room and board. In the math department at Maryland, I received a teaching assistantship to teach one course and to continue working on my PhD. My stipend was a handsome $115 per month. Thus, we were both students living near campus and eating all our meals at the student cafeteria. Margaret lived with friend of her mother's, and I found a room in a private home about a block away.

That arrangement lasted until Thanksgiving. The day before Thanksgiving, November 24, I picked up Margaret after her last class of the day, and we drove to Arlington, stopping at the florist to pick up a carnation boutonniere because we had miscounted the number of flowers to order previously. We were married at Community Methodist Church, in Arlington, Virginia. The marriage was rather informal, as Dr. Owens offered us the cash difference between a big formal wedding and a simple family affair. We took the cash—$2000. Her parents were pleased because it saved them the work of planning and doing the wedding, plus, they were assured that we had a bank account to start out.

My parents, Pearl and Calvin, flew out from Tucson, Arizona, and Dad was best man. Margaret's sister, Elizabeth, was maid of honor. A cousin of mine, Leroy Armstrong, and his wife, Dorothy, who lived in Laurel, Maryland, came. He took all the pictures with his professional equipment. We have beautiful pictures of the occasion, although of course, they are in black and white.

Margaret's mother had a reception at their house for a few close friends. She had ham and a wedding cake. It was raining when we drove off, so the rice that Elizabeth threw at the car stuck. We heard lots of honking as we drove through Washington, D.C. to our apartment in College Park, Maryland.

Our honeymoon time amounted to the weekend—Thursday, Friday, Saturday, and Sunday. We didn't go anywhere or spend any money for the "honeymoon." Monday it was back to school for us both. We moved into an apartment on Rowalt Drive just across the street from campus and near the cafeteria where we continued to eat. The small apartment had a living room, small kitchen, and a bedroom. It was three flights up, which was just good exercise for us. And the rent was cheaper than the lower floors—$72 a month. In the basement was a washer and dryer for the use of all the apartment renters. When Belva, Margaret's mother, visited, she arrived out of breath and exhausted. She was also horrified that Margaret would be carrying groceries all that way up.

With my small stipend of $115 and Margaret's $75 we were able to pay the rent and buy meal tickets (first semester) and food (second semester). The only other major expense I remember was some gas and insurance for the green grasshopper (Studebaker car). I mean we bought essentially nothing: no clothes, no furniture, no entertainment, no activities that weren't free. Each of us had our pre-wedding clothes. Furniture and kitchen utensils were discards from Margaret's mother, mostly from Margaret's childhood room. The furniture consisted of two twin beds (pushed together to make a sort of king bed), two maple chests of drawers, two card tables with two chairs, and several lamps. The card table was desk and dining table, so at meals the books, typewriter, and papers had to be moved. Pearl gave us a starter set of fiesta dishes as a wedding present. Margaret had bought a cedar chest from the classified ads to store her linens in. All of this furniture was in place before our wedding.

The University gave me a free activities book of coupons, and Margaret bought hers for $10. Therefore, our recreational activities were all school home athletic games, University play productions, and concerts, all of which came with our student activities pass. We attended all the home football games and basketball games and even gymnastics events and the like that were just available. We also occasionally drove to Margaret's parents for a Sunday dinner. We attended the local University Methodist Church and its young couples fellowship. The fellowship was mostly made up of folks like us who were in school. The designation of the group was C.C.C., which was supposed to stand for Christian Couples Club, but we decided it was Childless Couples Club. The only activity that went over was a monthly spaghetti dinner. The leaders tried to get us to go bowling or doing something else, but all we wanted to take time for was food.

All this time, Margaret was driving almost weekly to the Library of Congress in Washington, D.C. to work on her master's thesis on the children's book "Sing Song" by Christina Rossetti. She managed to finish her thesis and finish her Master's in time for the regular June graduation. She rented cap and gown to sit in the stands and stand en masse to receive her degree. She would have skipped the ceremony, as most of her comrades did, except that her parents wanted to be there to attend.

That summer, I taught summer school at the University, earning $400, which we promptly spent on a quick driving trip to Arizona. We stopped on the way at my cousin Bettie Anne Logan's house and saw her children Eddie and Joellyn and Randy. Returning from Arizona we drove frantically in order to be back in Maryland in time for cousin Kay Wolfe's August wedding to Dick Barrans. We broke speed limits driving to Baltimore for the wedding because we had arrived home late at night and overslept the day of the wedding. We slipped into the back of Towson Methodist Church and saw all the ceremony, but we didn't know that the Wolfes had planned for us to join them in the relatives section in the front.

In fall, I continued working at the University, still pursuing my PhD. Margaret took a teaching job in the local junior high, Hyattsville Junior High, teaching 7th grade "core." That "subject" was English, math, social studies, and science. Only art, music, and Phys-Ed were taught by other teachers. The teaching was complicated by the philosophy of the time, which promoted "democratic grouping." That meant that she had no one set of texts for every subject, and the students' reading abilities ranged from fourth grade to eleventh grade. She did a lot of oral work!

We continued to live in the apartment at Rowalt Drive. Thanks to Margaret's mother we acquired a dining room table, a cast off from one of her friends. It was that famous gate leg table that we have owned, and tried unsuccessfully to permanently pass on to children and grandchildren. That table went to Eileen in her first apartment, then back to us, then to Norman in his first apartment, and back to us, lastly to David Behm, our grandson, and was put in his apartment while he worked at a bank in Baltimore after his college graduation. We also bought a piece of furniture, a used highboy, which we still have and enjoy. It worked as file cabinet, and general storage.

To emphasize our bottom level of living, note the reaction of a local doctor. During her first year of teaching, Margaret caught flu or something that kept her in bed a few days. I called a doctor who came to see her. During his visit, I was in class, but he came and went, never sending us a bill for his services. The pharmacy delivered some medication, again without a charge. One look at our third floor apartment and the doctor knew our situation. That must have been why he never billed us. We discovered from a newspaper that we were living below the poverty line. However, we didn't feel poor, mostly because we knew that the situation was temporary, we were in good health (needing only contraceptives), and we had all our current needs covered . . . as long as our clothes and the car held out!

Carvel & Margaret, wedding 1954

CHAPTER 7

Beginning Professional Life and European Trip

During my second year in the Math Department of U. of MD, I was formally questioned by the math faculty for the level of Ph.D. It was rough, and most of my background was from other schools and other professors. The result was negative. I didn't meet their level of achievement for acceptance for Ph. D. This verdict was a crushing blow for me. I had passed the required language exams in both French and German, and taken the required number of courses. Anyway, I had to get a job.

That spring, 1956, at some sort of job fair, I interviewed with the chair of the Math Department of the U.S. Naval Academy, Professor Hawkins. He later offered me a job at the Naval Academy, which I accepted. I also applied for and interviewed for positions in the West, as I wanted to be near my parents, but nothing came through. Of course, I finished my teaching at Maryland with almost a full load that spring. I taught a number of the freshman math courses, including calculus.

June offered a needed break, and then my career at the Naval Academy formally began on July 1 of 1956. By July, Margaret and I had found an apartment in Annapolis on Constitution Avenue. It was up on the 2nd floor and less than a block from Annapolis High School (which is now Maryland Hall). The Junior High was next door to the high school, and of course within walking distance for Margaret. At that time schools were crying for teachers, so she had no difficulty securing a job at the junior high, again teaching seventh grade "Core." She was lucky to have a "Band" section. All her students were in Miss Harper's super band, and so were very smart kids. Down with democracy! To her surprise, she found that teachers were scared to teach the high level classes, fearing that the kids would know more than they did! Well, it took Margaret's kids about two months to figure out that they knew the times tables better than she did, but she had the answer sheet in the back of the book!

Our move from Rowalt Drive was interesting. I rented an open cart to hitch behind the "grasshopper." We filled that cart with our meager supply of furniture and took it all in one trip. Margaret made a number of trips in the car, carrying kitchen items and clothes before the "big" move. Our landlord lived practically next door in another of the apartments. He was one of the Brooks Brothers who had a hardware store on West Street in Annapolis. He gave us requested paint, and we repainted the walls in the bathroom, two bedrooms and kitchen. They went from plain plaster to yellow, blue, and green. Our rent was $75 a month—more than we had paid before. Also, another expense was we HAD to get a phone, at $5 a month. The Academy needed to be able to get in touch with us.

The Naval Academy was across town from us, but Annapolis is a small town, so I could walk the distance in a reasonable time. I did walk to work when there was snow on the roads, but usually drove the "grasshopper." Margaret had no transportation, but her school was easy to reach on foot. Those were the days of a ONE-car family. We remained a one-car family until February 1961.

The first year in Annapolis was enjoyable for us, and with two salaries we were able to save some money. My salary was $4,000, something, and less than $5000 a year. Margaret's salary was a princely $2,100. The $100 was the raise for having a year of teaching under her belt. The bad news about that salary was that social security payments went up, absorbing all of the increase in salary! The good news was that our living expenses were minimal. Anyway, we had enough cash to plan a big trip for the summer of 1957. We called it our honeymoon, since we hadn't traveled anywhere special after the wedding.

Carvel & Margaret, 1957 passport photo

We booked a two-month tour that specialized in European trips for college students. Technically, the tour left in early June, but Margaret's teaching didn't end that early. Most of the participants took a slow boat to England, but the tour booked us instead on the fast Queen Mary ocean liner out of New York to Southhampton. That crossing on the famous and great ship, Queen Mary, was a wonderful time for us. The ship had three classes: First, Cabin, and Tourist (AKA steerage!) When a passenger first arrived on the ship he could roam all over, but then he had to show up for lifeboat drill. While the passengers were at the drill, the crew shut all the doors between the sections of the ship, confining them to their appointed class. Our room was at the bottom of the ship, last deck down, nothing but bunk bed and sink. We shared a salt water shower down the hall. One had to make an appointment with the room steward to use the shower!

The ship had some entertainment for the tourist class, which we enjoyed: movies, crew led games. But the great fun was that we found the crew's staircase from the bottom, down in the hull, up to the first class decks. There, we went to the first class movie theatre, played ping-pong on the first class deck, and admired the swimming pool. We didn't have quite the daring to try to swim in the First Class pool, although the Tourist class had none. I think we got the "eye" from some of the crew and passengers, but had no trouble. No one was absolutely sure that we didn't belong. It was a five-day cruise on the Queen to England.

We were met at the harbor and put on a train to join our group at Stratford on Avon. The guide told us to just look out the window and get off at the right town. So we watched carefully as our train left London. We saw the station sign, "Way Out." OK. That was the first stop. It was an odd name, but Margaret figured some Brit had named a suburb because of it being so far from the center of town. The next station also had a big sign, "Way Out . . ." She was surprised, because with her extensive reading of novels set in London, she thought she should have heard of a suburb that large. The next station also had a big sign, "Way Out." About this time, we realized the sign meant "Exit." The station sign was not nearly as prominent, but considerably more informative!

We had a young man, probably in his 20's as our tour director. He made all of the arrangements, hotels, and meals and sightseeing. Our land travel was by bus, except crossing from England to Holland on a ferry. No tunnel then! The youth group, maybe 30 to 40 of us, filled the bus. All singles, except for us. We later discovered that Margaret had really made a faux pas. In a fit of feminist temper, she had made her reservation as a separate woman. So the poor tour director had to rush to the counter at each hotel and have the rooms rearranged because she and I were not booked together in one room. The tour people thought we were probably sister and brother.

We first saw a play in the Shakespearean theatre in Stratford on Avon. We ate in our bed and breakfast overlooking the Avon river, complete with swans. We saw Anne Hathaway's cottage. Then we traveled to London for several days, seeing the significant sights: London Tower with the crown jewels, Windsor Palace, Buckingham Palace with the famous changing of the guard, London Bridge, Downing street with the Prime Minister's House, Mme Tussard's Wax Works, etc.

There was time for shopping. We went to a china shop, and Margaret picked out a complete set of fine bone china, consisting of plates, cups, saucers, small plates, and bowls. The whole set was thoroughly packed and shipped to our home address. Naturally, we still have that set. It was 8 settings, and I know it is worth many times the price we paid! Indeed, we know, because when years later Margaret added to it to bring the settings to 12, the cost was enormous!

From London we bus toured the countryside, and then took a ferry across the channel to Holland-Amsterdam. In town, we went to the museums and saw the most famous paintings of Rembrandt and other classical artists. I particularly liked the fields of tulips, the bright countryside, with working windmills. Margaret bought a pewter pitcher as a souvenir. Everything was so new to us, who had never been outside the U.S.A. except for my tour in Panama.

From the fields of Holland we bussed into Belgium for a few days, and then through Luxemburg, on into Germany. There is a lot to see in Germany, so it took several weeks in that country. Germany was having a heat spell just as we went through. The students on our bus learned the word for swimming pool, and at every city, they hollered for "Swimbaad!" But a Swimbaad was not on the itinerary! We visited the great cathedral in Colon, the castles in Heidelberg, and along the Rhine. I especially remember staying near the junction of the Rhine and Mosel rivers. In particular, I went swimming in the Mosel river, of course downstream with the current and then walked back along the shore. We also had a boat ride past the famous Lorelei rocks at a bend in the Rhine River.

We continued by private bus into Switzerland seeing the high peaks, some snow covered. Our group stayed in Lucerne, near the beautiful late and visited the local sights. The next country, I believe was Austria, in particular the city of Vienna. There we heard something at the opera house and also toured the gorgeous summer palace, Schonbrun, outside of town in the country. The landmark palace at Versailles, France, was copied after the summer palace in Austria.

From there we continued down into Italy and spent many weeks in my favorite European country. It was also a country with a good exchange rate that year! I think that's why the tour spent so much time in it! The big sights were in Florence, with Michelangelo's statue of David, in Venice with its canals, in Rome with the coliseum and thousands of years of architecture, Pompey with its volcanic ruins, in Naples on the coast with a boat ride to the isle of Capri, in Pisa with the leaning tower, in Genoa the home of Columbus, and finally in Assisi, the town of St. Francis, and in so many lovely towns along the way.

Our bus followed the coastline through northern Italy over to France. We spent time in Monaco, the independent country on the Mediterranean Sea in the French Riviera region. NO, I didn't spend any money in the casino!

In fact, while we are on the subject of money, it was extremely tight. Those were the days before Visa. We carried cash and traveler's checks. And we had spent a bundle on the china purchase in London. We had been told to have "spending money," but we didn't realize that although the meals were provided, the BEVERAGES were not included. We had to order and separately pay for lemonade, or Coke with meals, other than breakfast, which usually included coffee. These beverages were often more expensive than the local wine! If one ordered water, it was likely to be fancy bottled water, not free tap water! No water was served with a meal. We were really rationing the cash by the end of the trip!

Although the year was 1957, and World War II had been over for about 12 years, I was warned that soap might be in short supply. We traveled with two small suitcases, but included powdered laundry detergent and a fold out rack for drying. Margaret washed underwear every place where stuff might dry, and we wore our outer clothes right through the summer. We survived.

Our tour continued north through the length of France to include Paris. We stopped in many cities along the way, including Avignon, and Chartres. In one little town we found a big celebration going on—parading of the local citizens, a gathering for speeches. Margaret, being short, began to edge her way to the front, and then, looking around, discovered that she was among the tallest of the local citizens! With a bit of French, she discovered that the citizens were celebrating the anniversary of their freedom from German occupation. Our bus driver, who was German, was hiding in the hotel all evening!

All the historic places were new, exciting, and eye opening to me. The only detraction in France was that many of the local tour guides conducted their spiel in French. Our tour guide tried to translate what was possible during the occasion. In every other country the local guides spoke in English.

Paris was The special place to visit: Sacra Coeur on the hill, Notre Dame Cathedral, museums, including the Louvre containing the painting of Mona Lisa, and of course the huge Eiffel Tower, near the Arc de Triumph.

Our group of students had spent two months together, from mid-June until mid-August so we had a fancy farewell banquet at a nice restaurant in Paris with gourmet food and farewells. From there, they all dispersed to their various travels home, except us. Margaret and I stayed on in Paris for most of another week until the next sailing of the Queen Mary out of Cherbourg, France.

That time for us was mostly walking around town, window shopping, and enjoying the ambiance of a different culture. We moved from the tour hotel to a low class cheap hotel and made do. Our guide book listed lots of place to eat, but it was August, "Les Vacances," and almost all of the stores and restaurants had closed for the universal vacation time.

A minor event of that week was my going to a barber for a professional shave. I had skipped shaving the entire two months and looked terrible, with a heavy beard—the only time of my life to let it grow. [Margaret adds: It was heavy in spots and not in others! Yes, it had nothing to recommend it. And the hair stayed scratchy the entire time. Who wants to kiss a scratchy face!]

We had round trip tickets on the Queen Mary and so took a train to the boat on the day of sailing. The voyage back across the ocean to

New York was very similar to the first crossing. As you can guess, we still sneaked into first class areas of the boat. During that time on shipboard, Margaret conceived, and our daughter, Cynthia, was born 9 months later on 3 May, 1958.

Remember, cash was very low. In fact, it was almost all gone. Fortunately we had in hand our return train tickets from New York to Washington, D.C. We realized that we were supposed to tip the crew of the Queen and we wondered how we could do that. Well, we attended one of the entertainments, a "horse race." One crew member threw the dice which indicated how far a given horse, pushed by another crew member, should go. "Our" horse won, paid off, and we immediately left the event with our small pot, which later went to the crew for their tip. Notice how the Lord provides.

When we arrived in New York, we discovered that the taxis were in short supply. We feared not getting one in time to ride to the train station to catch our ticketed train. I waved a half dollar and secured a taxi, although the driver insisted that he had been offered a dollar. Wow! He only got the 50 cent piece, because that was totally all I had in pocket.

The train brought us, penniless, with baggage to Washington. At Union Station, Dr. Owens, Margaret's father, picked us up for the drive to Margaret's original home in Arlington, VA. The "green grasshopper," our Studebaker, was parked there so we could drive to our apartment in Annapolis. A few weeks later our London china arrived safely and unbroken. What a memorable summer! Howver, a trip could not possibly be financially cut closer to the bone.

CHAPTER 8

First Years with the Navy

After returning from Europe, I went back to teaching, starting in August, at the Naval Academy in Annapolis. The Naval Academy was proud of its civilian faculty. Actually, the split between officers and civilians was close to 50-50. However, the civilian professors taught most of the academic classes, and military subjects like leadership and weapons were taught by regular military officers. Every midshipman was required to take mathematics at least the first two years. The first years I was there, every midshipman earned an engineering degree, but shortly after I came other majors were available. The majority of our students were in some phase of engineering, so you can guess the largest department was math. We had about 50 civilian professors and as many as 20 officers teaching in math, for a department of 70 full time teachers. Few college math departments came close to our size.

All of the officers teaching math had been to the Naval Post Graduate school, which had moved to Monterey, California. They had achieved the master's degree, at least. Actually, we had from time to time an officer who had gone all the way to PhD in mathematics. Our department was well known and well represented in the professional societies: The American Mathematical Society, and the Mathematics Association of America. I was a member of both fellowships.

Of interest, of course in those days ALL the students were male, all the teachers were male, and the midshipmen took their courses as units. That is a block of students gathered at Bancroft Hall, the dormitory, dining hall, recreation center for all of them, and marched to class. The students as a group had a schedule, not as individuals. They, naturally, wore uniforms. This policy changed gradually over the years until today students can major in many different areas, women are about 20% of each class, and the students stroll to whichever class is next on their individual schedule. One rule continues. All students take Physical education every year, and all students are required to participate in a varsity sport at 5 PM each day. The sports vary. There's swimming, volleyball, sailing, and pistol shooting besides the ones that you might think of. Every student must learn to swim. One of the requirements for graduation is to jump from the high diving platform, simulating abandoning ship in the ocean. The local newspaper reported one woman who was psychologically incapable of jumping that distance, despite the coaxing of swimming staff. She was about to be denied graduation because of this failure. However, I think someone intervened and allowed her to graduate anyway.

How did the inclusion of women change the academy? The comment of one spectator was, "It improved the college plays!" Prior to women midshipmen, the plays were either all male, like "Stalag 17," or drafted the young wives of the officers to take women's parts. Often the plays were Shakespeare plays because they called for few women.

The second year of my teaching, 1957-58, Margaret taught her seventh grade class in the fall at Annapolis Junior High. By Christmas she was noticeably pregnant and quit her teaching at the beginning of the Christmas holiday. We hosted at our apartment, December 15 the bridge party for the math department bridge group that we belonged to. Margaret had a "coming out" in recognition of her pregnancy by showing up in maternity clothing for the first time.

Cynthia, our first daughter, due May 5, came on May 3, 1958. In the meantime we were very busy looking for a house. I felt a "family" needed a home, rather than an apartment. We found a home south of Annapolis in Edgewater. Edgewater was a rural area on the Mayo peninsula, along South River, south of Annapolis. Our particular development was known as Loch Haven, about half way out the Mayo peninsula towards Chesapeake Bay. At the time, everyone in the math department thought we were out in the boon docks! We did have a tar and gravel road in front of us: called Riverside Drive, but the side roads were all dirt, and we had only a route and mailbox number for the postman—no house number.

I remember the closing ceremony in the lawyer's office. Our house was $21,000 and we put down as much as we could $5,000, to secure a better rate. The extra down payment got us a 5-½% loan, when most loans were 6% or more. Now, remember that we had just spent most of our savings on a trip to Europe. To scrape up that down payment Margaret cleared out her teacher's retirement fund, plus what she earned in the fall, Carvel took a loan from his parents for $1000, and we sold the stock that Carvel had bought with army severance pay. We also added the bi-weekly paycheck for that week. At the closing there were numerous taxes and fees and extra costs. I couldn't cover quite all of it, so I argued with the lawyers to lower fees. Actually the seller agreed to cover some of the costs, and I finally wrote a check on our bank account for the house balance that emptied my checking account. We walked out of that closing dead broke with nothing left but our clothes!

The closing was in April. We weren't eager to move immediately because of Margaret's pregnancy. The sellers, The Dunns, weren't eager to move because of children in school. So for two months they rented from us at a generous amount, I think about $400 a month, so they could stay on. Our mortgage payment was only $115 per month. The extra money made it possible for us to pay a mover to take our stuff to the new house. And to pay an exterminator to get rid of the army of fleas that the Dunns and their dog left behind!

Cynthia was born in Annapolis in the Anne Arundel General Hospital on Franklin Street. It was a one building hospital with air conditioners in the windows, and only street parking. I bumped into Dr. Borssuck, the GP who was Margaret's doctor, as I was walking into the hospital, and handed him the check to cover the charge for her delivery. I think it was about $1,000. [Margaret adds: I picked the doctor because he was in an office about one block from our apartment and he had office hours in the evening so I could go after school. He didn't take appointments and he didn't do much counseling. Carvel swore the doctor didn't get to the hospital in time to actually deliver Cindy—he stayed home until the nurses called him from the hospital three blocks away to tell him and Carvel that the baby was really on the way. When I went into labor, I was very slow. I babysat in the afternoon for a friend who was getting her hair done. Then I hung around the apartment all afternoon. At 5 PM Carvel insisted I should attend the bowling banquet ending the bowling season. So, rather than go to the banquet, I insisted he take me to the hospital. Carvel actually ate at his bowling banquet. When he told the others why I wasn't there, they gave him the centerpiece bouquet to take to me, so he delivered it to the hospital later.

I was in delivery from about 6 PM to early morning when Cindy finally arrived. When Carvel showed up at the hospital, later in the afternoon, I chided him for not being there when I came out of delivery. It turned out he had been there, had held my hand as I was wheeled from delivery to my room, but because of the anesthesia effects, I didn't remember. I also kept asking the nurse if I had had a boy or a girl, and couldn't remember the answer for hours. You know there were no x-rays or sonograms done in those days.)

Margaret stayed in the hospital about four days. She and her roommate were having a great time together. She did cross stitching on hand towels as a gift for her mother. When I picked up Margaret and Cynthia at the hospital, Margaret carried the baby in her arms all the way to her parents' home in Arlington, VA. There was an old wives' tale that whoever carried the baby home from the hospital would be the person that the baby most resembled. HMMM. Of course no one was so cruel as to put the new baby in a cold hard container. But later on, the baby rode in the bassinet set loosely on the back seat. There were no baby seats or seat belts at that time. Note the huge difference today! Babies were identified in the hospital by a bracelet made of tiny beads with the parent's last name on it. Margaret kept that bracelet for a long time.

While she was at her parents, Margaret learned how to pin cloth diapers on a baby. It was a big experiment because Margaret's mother had had a maid doing all that stuff, so she didn't know the technique either. The diapers pins were big and a bit scary. One always feared piercing the baby. Neither of them had seen an umbilical cord. What was one supposed to do? Margaret had no trouble nursing, though she had feared having small breasts might be a problem. Having a baby over the weekend at a hospital is not the way to go because the nurses are few. However, the rep from the state got there in time to register the baby's birth, and the photographer managed to picture the new baby—a couple of days after birth.

That year we lived from pay check to pay check, just managing to eat and pay the mortgage—which was half of my take-home pay. [If you are curious, our mortgage payment was $115 per month—all of one paycheck each month. We had two pay checks each month, the second for living expenses.] It's a miracle that we had no extra expenses except pediatrician—whose office visit was $5. The house echoed for lack of rugs, and only the living room, dining room, and our bedroom had furniture. Our bedroom still sported twin beds from Margaret's childhood pushed together as one bed, plus her childhood chests of drawers. Cindy's room had a crib that Margaret's parents had given us. The living room had a new playpen and a cast off sofa from Margaret's parents. We moved into the new home in June, after the Dunns moved out to Florida.

[Margaret notes: Carvel had a summer job. He bragged later that he helped build the Naval Academy stadium—he worked part of that 1958 summer as a carpenter's helper. That same summer we moved he also had a job with the surveyor's office in Annapolis. He plotted on a map the measurements that the men in the field brought in. He continued to hold summer jobs, in later years at Johns Hopkins teaching math, until we discovered that he had completed 40 quarters of social security payments and would qualify for minimum social security payments in retirement. At age 65 he filed for the payments and began receiving them—about $75 per month. The main benefit of the social security has been the Medicare benefit. However in 2010, he received a bill because his benefits were too small to cover the cost of the Medicare—the deductions exceeded the benefit!] Fortunately, social security was just a small extra to my retirement. The main retirement is my government check from 36 years of contributions to their retirement program while teaching at the Naval Academy. I had an extra generous retirement rate, no longer available, that pays me about 2/3 of my final salary, plus cost of living increases. The retirement rates were changed not many years after my employment and are far less today. When the new changes were made, I and others were allowed to keep our original retirement agreement which went 'way back to the depression years of the 1930's. The expected life span at that time was about 65 years, so the government didn't envision paying out for very long! I, praise the Lord, got the best of the best, as probably the last one hired under the old rate agreement. The next civilian professor hired in the math department was close to ten years after me, and was certainly under the reduced program.

The driveway at our new house was brown gravel with a strong slope downward to the community road. We always drove around on the flat public road and then into the driveway and then down hill to leave. It was nice that the driveway crossed the front yard from the side street, at that time named Holly Drive, (later McAfee Rd.) to the main road, then called Riverside Drive, but later South River Terrace. We made the driveway one way, downhill because you couldn't drive up the hill if there was any snow or ice, and if you drove up it in warm times, you spewed gravel out of place under your wheels. But I could drive down hill in any snow less than a foot. As for shoveling, only the top for a short distance needed to be cleared as long as the side road was plowed. We had to make a sharp turn to enter the carport, which was on the side of the house, and later converted into a sunroom.

Of course, the weeds grew through the gravel, so I was always pulling weeds in the driveway as well as around the lawn. It was a big job to keep that corner lot in good shape. The first thing necessary was to chop out several huge stumps of trees that had been cleared.

For many years, I planted flowers and azaleas around the house. It seemed appropriate to increase the flower bed across the front on the opposite side of the driveway. The previous owners had planted black tulips there, which survived a few years. A retired professor from the math department, Prof. Epps, had started a nursery with several greenhouses in his yard. I visited and he gave me several dozen daffodil bulbs and three iris tubers to get my garden started. Well, those daffodil bulbs and iris tubers grew and divided many times over the years. We did buy a few more daffodil species, but most of the bulbs came from the starters. In 50 years, I had over 1,000 blooming daffodils in my yard—all around the four sides of the house, and in all our neighbor's yards. Of course, they bloom in the spring, just before the azaleas, which I also put all around the house. Margaret picked up the first three red azaleas and the first two white azaleas, tiny things that would fit in your hand, for 25 cents at Murphy's "5 and 10" in downtown Annapolis across from City Dock. Our place was the local show place every spring.

I had a wild, volunteer, dogwood tree, which had escaped mowing because it grew out of the stone terrace on the side of the yard. Later, we went into the woods and transplanted two small dogwoods into the "front triangle." They both survived for many years until one year one of them just died. Also, in the front triangle we planted, from the woods, two small holly trees, hoping that one would be female and give berries. Well, one was, and years later, when they began to crowd each other, the male came down. The female kept on with berries—no trouble with pollination. The berried branches supplied us with Christmas decorations, and in February, the robins would come in flocks and eat all the fruit in a day or two. They were like a cloud of locusts.

On the side of the house beside the carport, the previous owner had planted a small oak tree. We took it out and put in a five graft apple tree. It was supposed to produce apples at five different times, which in theory was great. However, some of the grafts weren't as vigorous as others and nearly died out. The other grafted parts bloomed at slightly different times, requiring different spraying times. If I didn't spray, the apples were impossible. Then, we wound up with more apples than we really wanted as the tree grew. After the children were grown and gone, and the tree was past its best bearing time, Carvel dug it up, "pruned it down to the ground," and we planted a crepe myrtle in its place.

Out back, I put in a vegetable garden that gave us fresh lettuce, tomatoes, beans, Swiss chard, beets and rhubarb all those 50 years. That garden was just big enough for the family—about 10 feet by 20 feet. Over those 50 years, the ground improved from solid clay to lovely loamy soil after the continual addition of compost, mulch, and fertilizers.

Also out back when we left, was our patio, a wood pile by the terraced wall, and a compost pile for all the leaves and discarded vegetable matter. At first, right behind the house was just dirt. A neighbor, just across the street, with a young boy who had outgrown the equipment, gave us an outdoor "climbing tower." It had a swing, trapeze bar, and ladders on four sides to the top, about 8 feet up. Our children played on that set for many years while they were growing up. It stayed over the bare dirt-grass, until it rusted out.

As the children grew up, we improved the play area. About that time, my parents visited from Tucson, Arizona and Dad, Grandpa Wolfe, bought a basketball along with the basket and backboard. Growing out of the stone retaining wall was a wild cherry tree. It was at least two feet in diameter, with large limbs over the yard. After removing the lower limbs, we hung the backboard on the trunk of that cherry tree at the far edge of our lot. Well, we found out that you can't bounce a ball on grass, and the grass gave way to mud. So, we had to contract for a cement slab. Margaret thought that basket was a rather expensive gift! When we had the slab put in, we had the man put a metal sleeve in the center for a post for tetherball. Because of our small lot, not many ball games were possible, but tetherball was. In the game you batted the ball with your hands to wind it up on the pole—a two-person game. As the children grew up, we improved the play area. By the time they reached junior high level, now called middle school, we had a cement contractor expand the cement area so we could put a picnic table out there.

My Dad helped me hang a swing on ropes from a high limb on the cherry tree. Everybody could swing in a large arc. On down the stone wall beyond the slab, were a number of other volunteer trees, all growing out of that stone wall. From one of those trees I hung a large rope, maybe 2 inches in diameter, as a climbing rope. You could climb up the rope some 15 feet or so to the limb. One incident before the installation of the rope: My son, Norman, was a determined climber who would climb anything. He climbed that tree up to near the top where the limbs were too thin to hold him. He was maybe 5 years old. The limb broke! Grandpa was watching down below and caught him in his arms in mid-air. Now you see why I hung the rope! Eventually I took all the trees out of that wall except the big cherry and the dogwood beside the house.

Speaking of trees, I also planted a peach tree, a pear tree, and another apple tree on the bedroom side-west of the house. The peach tree did a marvelous job of supplying us with top-notch peaches for almost 50 years. For most of those years, we canned 50 or more quarts of peaches each August. Those canned peaches lasted us a good part of the winter as breakfast fruit with cereal. During harvest, the latter part of August, we ate fresh peaches all three meals every day. In fact the fresh peaches lasted through September. I had so many peaches that I gave a heaping bucket to a half dozen neighbors.

The apple tree also provided quantities of apples. We stashed lots of apples in the basement refrigerator. We pestered the children to eat apples after school. Margaret made applesauce of most of the apples and canned the sauce. The apples never looked good enough to give away. The pear tree died after a few years from fire blight. The apple tree on the bedroom side of the house developed a root fungus and had to be cut down. I sprayed the peach tree at all the right times every spring and summer and kept the peaches coming.

In addition to all the flower beds and azaleas around the house, I put in a rose garden across the back. In season, we had beautiful roses on the table as a weekly event. [Margaret adds: Every Fall, about August, Carvel would come in the house with a rosebud, and announce, "This is the Last Rose of Summer." Then a week or two later, he would bring in another bud and repeat, "This is the Last Rose of Summer," because the roses lasted longer than we thought they would!]

I've gotten 'way ahead of myself in talking about the yard over the years. Let's go back to the family and the house. Cynthia was the prime attraction those first two years—1958-1960. Margaret took care of the baby and I taught at the Academy. [Margaret adds: In case you're interested, I nursed each of my children for 6 months, which was considered by the doctors to be the optimum time, and switched them to a cup at that time and regular cow's milk. I was rather afraid of sterilizing bottles and convinced that God had a plan when he gave mothers milk. It was later that I heard that nursing was really great for children, giving them all sorts of special immunities and such. Almost no mothers nursed their children when I was doing it. I would say to the pediatrician that I was worried about some situation. The doctor would sigh, and say, "I guess we could change the formula." I'd say, "But I am nursing!" Then he'd respond, "Then everything's just fine!" That response was very reassuring to me.]

In June of 1960 our second daughter, Eileen, was born. [Margaret adds: While I was pregnant, Carvel refused to consider female names and urged me to wear blue. He really hoped for a boy. I had been running girl names by him, after all we'd chosen a girl's name two years ago. But nothing was decided. The morning after I delivered—I always managed to deliver on weekends and at night—the social worker was in the room to fill out the birth certificate and wanted a name. I had personally selected Eileen, and so I told her to use that name on the certificate. A few hours later, Carvel bounced into the hospital room and said, "I guess we'll have to select a girl's name." He was rather chagrined to hear that she was already officially named. We carried Eileen home in my arms about three days later.]

[Margaret continues: Carvel doesn't remember this part, but I do. When Cindy was born, Carvel drove me directly from the hospital to my parents' house in Arlington. I stayed for maybe a week, and then came back to our apartment and Pearl Wolfe came and kept house for a couple of weeks. When Eileen was born, again Carvel drove first drove Cindy to my parents' home. However, they were just about ready to move to Los Angeles. I think they delayed a bit so they could see me through for a while. When I left the hospital, he drove me and Eileen to join them and be taken care of. The incident I remember most, and the one I have tried to forget was something Elizabeth, my sister, did. My mom, Elizabeth, and I and two-week-old Eileen were all in the living room. Eileen was in the bassinet, crying. I was too tired to do anything, and inclined to let her cry away. Elizabeth thought she'd comfort the baby and picked Eileen up. Unaccustomed to babies, she didn't support Eileen's head, which wasn't so much of a problem until she went to sit down. It wasn't a "sit," it was a drop down. Poor little Eileen's head jarred and she screamed. I grabbed her and clenched my teeth lest I say something regrettable, and dashed into another room where I walked with the baby until she calmed down. However, there was neck damage. For six months or so, Eileen kept her head turned to one side. We feared for brain damage and serious side effects. At one point the doctor thought she was retarded. I guess time proved that she recovered, but I found it hard to forgive Elizabeth for hurting my baby.]

With two tots, my wife was really tied down. [Margaret interjects: You don't know the half of it. I had just toilet trained Cindy, and I had cloth diapers to deal with again. It meant laundry every day. Although

Carvel's parents, Pearl and Calvin, had given us an automatic clothes washer, a Bendix, we had no dryer. I had to hang clothes outside all day and bring them back in later in the afternoon before the dew settled. In rainy weather, I strung the clothes on lines in the basement. In good weather, Cindy would be outside with me and she was determined to play in the stones in the front driveway while I hung clothes out back. I had to keep chasing her and bringing her back to the back yard because in the driveway she was too close to the road and I wouldn't be able to see her there. In addition, I had no transportation as we had only one car. I had to plan ahead for the car, which meant making appointments on Carvel's day off or driving him to the academy, coming home with the car, and then driving in later to pick him up after work. The one activity we could do was walk around Loch Haven, and walk to the beach in summer. Fortunately, the library ran a van to the community at a specified time each week, so we could check out books. About that time, my parents closed the house in Arlington and moved to Los Angeles—San Marino. They gave us their old black and white TV set. With a TV set, we were enthralled. After the kids were down, we watched everything. We had THREE channels to choose from. What luxury!]

Carvel continues: At least I got home early, often 3 or 4 in the afternoon. So I did get a chance to romp and play on the floor with the little ones. About that time, for extra money, I taught a night class twice a week at the Johns Hopkins University. It was a long hour drive each way from home to the center of Baltimore. It was made a little easier because I could carpool from Parole with several other Naval Academy professors who were doing the same thing. I got home from Hopkins just in time to go to bed. It certainly was good that I had boundless energy.

For exercise at work, every day I went to the Academy pool during the lunch break. I swam 20 laps or 500 yards each time along with a daily shower. I only needed to shower at home on weekends. [Margret notes: He mentions that because with my daily water use for clothes washing, we had septic problems. The ground couldn't absorb as much water as we were putting into it.] Amazingly, I also had time to eat lunch in the math department lounge in just a few minutes. Margaret packed me sandwiches, a piece of fruit, and a slice of home-baked cake [Margaret says: without icing, I might add—too much trouble] in the famous brown bag. Almost everybody had brown bags from the grocery store. There was also a small thermos for drink. In our faculty lounge, where I ate, was a refrigerator for keeping the carried lunches. Many of the faculty went out to eat, at the officer's club, or elsewhere. I was right there in the mathematics building for lunch and could get to class in a couple of minutes. Actually, I tried to get schedules with either a fourth or a fifth period off so that I wasn't so pushed in eating. There were 4 periods of classes in the morning, 7:45 to 11:45, and 2 periods in the afternoon, 1:15 and 2:15. Each class went for 50 minutes. My teaching load was normally 3 or 4 classes per day. The administration tried to average 3 classes, so that after a semester of 4 classes, you could expect a light schedule of only 2 classes. Of course, we were expected to hold office hours for students and to do our own research, along with administrative duties. You were busy all day, but even with a sixth period class, you were out by 3:05 in the afternoon. For the first couple of years, I also had Saturday morning classes. But soon the administration decided to schedule only military classes on Saturdays.

I continued to drive the old 1950 Studebaker, "grasshopper," up until the mid 1960's. Margaret had no car or transportation before 1961. She stayed home except when I had a day off. Somehow, she got babies to the doctor's office when necessary for shots or earaches and colds. We both picked up groceries and necessities. I brought milk home from the High's store in Edgewater several times a week. [Margaret interjects: In fact, Carvel bought almost all the groceries, shopping in an Acme on Rowe Blvd. Annapolis. There was no grocery store closer to us than that. Going grocery shopping was a delight if I could do it by myself. If I had kids along, it was miserable.

I remember one time I phoned Carvel and left a message for him to bring home 2 pounds of salt. I wanted to make a relief map with the kids. Carvel got the message, but there were a couple of practical jokers in the faculty and all the professors shared one big room, so jokes were readily known. He knew that we wouldn't normally use two pounds of salt in ten years—it had to be a practical joke—so he skipped that purchase, only to discover that I really wanted that salt.]

We got along without buying anything in the way of clothes or furniture, except kids clothes. Margaret shopped out of the Sears Roebuck catalog. We did have the black and white TV that was given us by Margaret's parents. The children watched Captain Kangaroo and that was about it for them.

*   *   *

Margaret's Snow Story

Whenever a group begins to tell of occasions when they had a snow experience, I, Margaret, have a story that tops them all. This is my story:

It was February of 1961. Carvel and I had decided that after 2 ½ years of living in the boondocks of Edgewater, we both needed and could afford a second car. I had had to make special plans whenever I had to take Cindy, age 2 ½, or Eileen, age 8 months, to the doctor. Our usual routine was that I would pack the girls in the car and drive Carvel to the Academy. Then at the end of the school day I had to pack them in again to drive and pick him up at work. He did the grocery shopping. I shopped via Sears and Roebuck catalog for most other items. It was not very convenient.

The midshipmen were allowed to buy cars their first class (senior) year, and they had a committee, which negotiated a good price for the various cars that the men were interested in. As a faculty member, Carvel could take advantage of this negotiated price. The low bid for the Mercury Comet that we wanted was a dealer in Washington D.C. So we drove in one afternoon, ordered the car, and plunked down the price in a personal check, plus three or four tiny dividend checks. Of course the dealer wanted to check that all these checks were good, so we were to return the next week for the car.

On the appointed day, a Thursday, I believe, I piled the girls in the green Studebaker and drove Carvel to work. Then in the afternoon at 2, the three of us drove to pick Carvel up to head for the dealership. On the way, we heard the radio announce that Washington was getting two inches of snow. Two inches wasn't enough to create a problem, we thought. But we hadn't heard all the news. By the time we reached Washington, the snow was piling up to over six inches and still falling. The Federal Government was letting employees out early. Traffic was bad and nightfall was not far off.

We pulled into the dealership. The salesmen were standing around watching the snow come down. They looked at us in astonishment. "What are YOU doing here?" "Well," we explained, "We said we'd come today, and here we are." The salesmen sprang into action (they had nothing else to do anyway), ordering the mechanics to get the car ready as quickly as possible. They hadn't really expected us to be there. There were papers to sign, and then we headed out in two cars.

The Studebaker had little tire chains that Carvel could strap on, which he did. He put me and the girls in the Studebaker because he figured with chains the car would be sure to get through. He drove the new car, counting on the new tire tread to grip the road enough to handle the snow. As a precaution, he had me drive in front so that if I got stuck he would be behind to help. We headed out.

Cars were stuck in the ice on one small hill on the highway going out of town. Some good Samaritan men were pushing the cars up the road to the top level. Each of our cars was pushed up and then we were on the highway. The snow was still falling and visibility was almost nothing.

I had to make one turn at an intersection to get onto Route 50, which was the main highway toward our house. In the snow and unfamiliar territory, I missed the turn, drove across the highway and into a residential section. I heard honking, which I found out later was Carvel trying to tell me to turn around, but the honking just scared me into driving faster. Well, when I realized I was no longer on a major road, it was impossible to turn around. I thought I'd better not stop and drive into a driveway because I'd lose my momentum and not be able to start again. So I kept driving, looking for a cross street to enable me to return to the highway. There were no tracks in the snow other than the ones I was making. Finally, the street which I was on seemed to swing around to the left, so I could hope that it would lead me back. Then on a small, completely snow covered hill, my car slid to the right into a ditch and I was stuck.

I sat for a minute in the car. I'd heard too many stories of people freezing to death in cars, or dying of carbon monoxide because of attempting to keep the engine running. I knew I had to get help. I stepped out of the car. I told Cindy to stay there, and that I'd be back. I left her watching over Eileen drowsing in her baby basket on the back seat. I stepped out of the car and looked at the houses. There were four houses in sight, two on the left and two on the right. The houses looked much alike, two-story Colonials, lights in the windows, but absolutely no footsteps or car tracks anywhere.

For some unknown reason, I decided to try first the second house on the right. I walked up, through the snow, knocked on the door and waited. A middle-aged couple opened the door a crack. They saw, on their doorstep, a young woman, 27 years old, with a round innocent face asking for shelter in the storm. This woman, they saw, had no snow boots, an inadequate coat, and no hat as snow protection. The man glanced over my head at the snow still coming down and the unplowed street, and opened the door a bit wider. "I guess you can't get to a motel in this weather, and no snow plows will be available. So you can stay here." He stepped back to let me come in.

Then I had to tell him, "I have two children in the car, a toddler and an infant." He looked at me in astonishment. But he grabbed his coat to help me bring the children in. He carried two-year-old Cindy, and I carried the baby basket with Eileen in it. As we returned to the house, he glanced at the neighboring house to his. "You walked past their house to get to ours!" Then he breathed, "They probably wouldn't have let you in."

Anyway, we wound up in their cozy kitchen at the kitchen table. The lady whipped out peanut butter and jelly and made sandwiches for me and Cindy to feast on. Eileen could drink milk out of a cup (when I held it), and lo and behold, the family had strained baby food. It turned out that the husband had a stomach ulcer, which in those days was treated with soft foods.

Settled for the night into the den on the couch, with Cindy in a "nighty" of a man's t-shirt, I began to try to reach Carvel to tell him that we were all right. I phoned and phoned. The phone in our house rang and rang, but no one answered. You see, I had the old car, and on the car key ring were the house keys. I had the ONLY house keys. Finally, at eleven o'clock, I gave up calling and went to sleep.

The next morning, I reached Carvel, who was frantic and had the police out looking for me. I got towed and headed home. Later, I discovered that Norman shared this adventure with us because I was pregnant.

Anyway, I later got Carvel's side of the story. He watched in frustration as I drove ahead of him onto a side road. He was the one who honked at me. He waited at the intersection, in a gas station lot, expecting me to come back any minute when I realized my mistake. When I didn't return, he decided I'd probably gone around a block and returned to the highway at a different point. He drove home, expecting to find my car in the driveway. It wasn't there of course. He couldn't get into the house, so he went to a neighbor's house to watch our driveway. At eleven o'clock, he had imposed on the neighbors enough, so he broke into the house via the back door. Remember, I gave up calling at eleven o'clock. No one had answering machines or cell phones then, so he had no news. He called the police, but couldn't tell them where to look for me. After a rocky night, when I still hadn't arrived home, he called the office at school and pleaded family emergency in order to stay home and wait for news. That's why, in the morning, I could reach him by phone and tell him we were ok. And, thanks to God and some good people, we were.

Whenever I can do a good turn for someone I do, because I remember that a very good turn was given to me in an emergency.

Carvel continues: It was mostly from this experience and others, I had an extra key to the front door made and put it into a metal magnetic box. That box remained behind a stand-up pipe in the back of our house for all the rest of our years there. Actually, I used that key several times over the many subsequent years.

In 1961, September 9, just a little more than a year after Eileen arrived, my son Norman was born. I remember my parents in Tucson were shocked. Mom, Pearl, advised me strongly not to have any more children! Well, the truth is, we were happy to have three as enough. With a son and two daughters, we had an exceptionally nice family that has been a joy ever since.

[Margaret confides: OK. This is the inside story. It's a secret. Remember, I nursed Eileen for 6 months. Nursing is a sort of contraceptive. But I was using a diaphragm with a spermicidal jelly. The problem I later figured out was that the jelly was left over from before Eileen, so it was over a year old, and apparently had lost its oomph. In addition, I was so tired, I had gone to a local doctor and she had prescribed thyroid pills, which did indeed pep me up. When I next saw her, I told her I'd have to quit the thyroid pills because of pregnancy. She grinned a bit, and said, "The other woman I gave thyroid pills to also reported getting pregnant!" I told her that we did want another child, just not quite so soon. And, although I said that, I really was in dark gloom. For several months I moped about, barely paying attention to Eileen and Cindy.]

My mother, Pearl, came to Loch Haven after the birth of each child, and stayed a number of weeks to help out Margaret as she recovered. Pearl was a big help with the children so Margaret could get some rest. [Margaret adds: Norman's due date was late September, but he came early. I went into false labor on September 3, and so Pearl moved her plane flight up to be here in time. She was here when I went to the hospital September 8, and knew some of the routines. The doctor kept me in the hospital for almost a week to rest. The nurses would go off duty and come back on and say "Are you still here?!" Pearl kept asking what I wanted her to cook or to do, and I wanted her to just decide. The washing machine had to run every day with those diapers for two babies. The Bendix machine was a sort of squeeze box, a gift from Pearl and Calvin, who sold Bendix washers and appliances to retail outlets in Arizona. My machine was giving out when Pearl was there. She couldn't understand why, as hers had been good for about 6 years. Then she realized, at home she did one load a week, and at my house I did 6 loads a week. Those cloth diapers, by the way, were around the house for umpteen years as good rags.)

[Margaret continues: Carvel told me that as he was leaving the hospital, marveling that he had three children, he realized that he had three children and the oldest was three! Eileen and Norman were 15 months apart. Later, it was like having twins because Norman's size caught up to Eileen's when they were about 2 and 3.] They actually looked like twins!

Christmas, 1961, was memorable with 3 little ones, age 3 ½, 1 ½, and ½. Margaret made handprints of each child. She cut them out of green paper and mounted them on a white sheet, arranged like a Christmas tree. She cut their names out of folded paper so that they came out like mirror images, and used that for the stem of the tree. She sent them to both sets of grandparents. The Wolfe's in Tucson framed it, and we have that picture hanging on our wall today as a hand-me-down from my parents.

[Margaret remembers: I had joined the local Loch Haven Garden Club—because I could walk to the meetings and the initial one was in the evening when Carvel could baby-sit. 1961 the club decided that we should promote Christmas decorations by having a contest in the community. Each of us was to set an example by putting up a decoration. So that was the year that I designed the Madonna and child cut out for our picture window. Carvel bought the plywood sheet. I drew it. He cut it out with a little handsaw, and I painted it. That year we received a little bowl for first prize in the religious category. The first year the painting was tempera, but we later decided to hang it outside, and I had to paint it in more durable paints, and even cover it with Valspar varnish to protect it from rain. We hung that same painting every Christmas season for 50 years, with old style large lights strung around the window like a Christmas card, and a spotlight on it.]

The summer of 1962, in June after school was out, we flew as a family to Tucson to visit for a month or two. We bought only 2 ½ plane tickets. We had two lap babies, Norman in Margaret's lap, and Eileen in mine. Cindy had a seat, but it was half price. However, tickets cost more then. I think it was close to $1,000 for the plane fare. The plane changed in Dallas, Texas, and then landed on a runway in Tucson. [Margaret remembers: We were sitting in a family area against the bulkhead with facing three-person benches. When the meal was served, the stewardess placed a pillow on the person's lap, and then the meal tray on the pillow. Well, with a lap baby, I couldn't eat. Carvel had Cindy give her seat to Eileen, and Cindy sat on the floor for a while. You know there were no seat lap belts in those days. Carvel and the older children managed to eat. The gentleman in the facing chair across from us ate quickly, and then took Norman on his lap while I ate. When we were in Texas, the man walked Cindy out of the plane for a little break. He was, I believe, Christian Scientist and referred to children as little angels and heavenly light. I rather thought he didn't have any children or he might have had another opinion. But I wasn't about to argue.]

In Tucson, there were no terminal connections. We walked from the plane on the runway to the terminal carrying babies. How nice it was to be young and strong, so that no amount of inconvenience bothered us! From 1962 until 1978, we traveled to Tucson on an every other year basis. On the even years we were there, and on the odd years, my parents drove to Loch Haven to see us. Those summer trips to Tucson turned out to be major cross-country sightseeing tours. From Tucson, we drove on to LA in California to visit Margaret's parents, the Owens. Dr. Owens retired from the faculty of George Washington U in 1959 and relocated in San Marino, a suburb of L.A. He immediately took a teaching job in the University at Long Beach, and kept teaching business administration for many years until he was in his mid 70's.

CHAPTER 9

Raising Children

The three children got along exceptionally well, partly because they were so close in age. I already mentioned that first summer, 1962, when we all crowded into three seats on planes to Tucson for a visit. My mom, Pearl, took pride in trying to fatten us up with her good cooking. Of course, she had been trying that on me for over thirty years without success. Anyway, it was a joy to be pampered. Especially nice was Dad's fresh game from hunting. We ate dove breasts and wild javalina (pig) that my father had shot out in the desert. On a few occasions he shot a duck or even a deer. Those animals were rare around the Tucson hills.

I tried out Dad's shotgun, but couldn't hit a dove. They were too fast. Dad was a very good golfer—played every week. He tried to teach me on the summers that we visited. Golf also wasn't my game. We enjoyed the walks. Dad also shot several large diamondback rattlesnakes out in the rough. This was before killing a rattlesnake became illegal. He skinned those snakes, cured the skins in brine, and tanned the hide. With the skins, he made belts by mounting the beautiful diamond pattern on a leather base. Finally, he attached a pure silver buckle, which was made in Mexico. Dad wore one of the belts and gave me the other. Now I have both belts and prize them above any financial value. They are irreplaceable because you can't kill a rattlesnake today.

When we were in Tucson, the children could play in a park just half a block away. Pearl tried to introduce the kids to what she considered good music, which was the Lawrence Welk Show. They would plead to be excused to go play in the playground.

Pearl and Calvin tried to save a few of the grapefruit on the grapefruit tree in their back yard so that the kids could have the experience of picking the fruit They also grew a grapevine on an arbor. The grapes were usually ripe when we came, and we delighted in eating them. Pearl and Calvin were tired of eating the grapes and tried to "fancy" them up by putting them in Jell-O or some salad, but we liked them best plain.

Back home, all five of us thrived. Margaret did a wonderful job with the children. She read to them every day, using every children's book that came in the mobile library. She also got books from the local Annapolis library because she now had transportation. The Edgewater library hadn't been built yet. Groceries had to come from an A & P on West Street in Annapolis. The children knew the stories of Dr. Seuss. They could repeat the story as you turned the page.

Margaret saw that all 3 were dressed in the best. Once a year she hired a babysitter so she could attend the dramatic sale at "Lad and Lassie," the top fashion store for kids in downtown Annapolis. That was in addition to the catalogs. Annapolis had no other stores except the brand new shopping center in Parole—Britts, Stride Rite Shoes, and Woodward and Lothrop.

A small aside about Britts: As a promotion for the opening, the store offered some items free by a lottery. Margaret and I went to check if our number, sent to us in the mail, was on any of the goods, and lo and behold, our number was in the rug department. We could have a free carpet installed. Margaret picked out the color, and the workmen came out to measure. Remember, all the employees were totally new. The woman who came to visit Margaret and show rug samples was wearing a hat with the price tag still dangling, and her main conversation centered around how unhappy she was that she had to work! The men miss-measured the master bedroom floor space. So the delivered carpet wouldn't fit. So, we said, "Since you have to re-cut, how about we order a better grade of carpet." So that was ok. Then they didn't figure it right again, and had to take the carpet back and re-cut it. We finally got a blue-gray carpet down in the master bedroom, and it stayed down until the day we left the house about 50 years later. When we finally pulled up the carpet, we discovered that the installers had stapled all over the padding, ruining the oak hardwood floor beneath, and had randomly used tape without any sense of where the tape should have been placed. What ignoramuses!

Those "ka-boop-ers," as I called the children, could read rather well before entering first grade. There were no public kindergartens at that time, so Margaret enrolled each child at the appropriate age in Mrs. Phillips' private kindergarten. Each morning she drove to the kindergarten held in Mrs. Phillips' home down Muddy Creek road, and off on a side road. Actually for Cindy there was a carpool—with Wendy Buss and Peg Long's child. With Eileen, one of the Creighton boys was going too. Mrs. Phillips had "tests" that a child had to learn to "pass." Each skill rated a check on a chart. One skill was to be able to tie shoes. Another was to know your parents' proper names. Then there was being able to recite your address and phone number. You had to know your colors and be able to count to ten, or maybe a hundred. You were also expected to recognize your name. Margaret thinks the kids learned their letters too, but Mrs. Phillips said she was not allowed to teach reading— that skill was reserved for first grade teachers. Margaret used to drop the child off and try to get to the grocery store, back home, unload the groceries, and then back to pick up child. Sometimes she was late, but she usually arrived in time. Kindergarten ran from 9 to 11:30 I think.

It was also at this time that Cindy, aged 5, was diagnosed with allergy reactions. She had constant "colds" which turned into earaches that the pediatrician had to treat with antibiotics. The allergist did a scratch test on Cindy's back and determined that she was allergic to dust, pollen, smoke, and feathers. We drove home, stopping on the way for polyester pillows and dumped the feather pillows we had all been using in the garbage. They had been inherited from Margaret's grandparents, anyway. Cindy had shots three afternoons a week to desensitize her. That kept Margaret in the doctor's office an awful lot of time, with the other two children tagging along. However, the change in pillows made the most difference. And Norman, who had been having colds too, cleared up since he no longer had a sick sister sitting beside him.

I remember so well what went on at home after Cynthia started first grade. We had a small child's table with tiny chairs in the girls' bedroom. As soon as she came in, Cynthia plopped sister Eileen and brother Norman down at that table in front of the chalkboard and taught the first grade lesson. I don't think Eileen had any choice. Since Eileen was two years younger, she was rather over whelmed with the heft of the lesson.

When Eileen's turn finally came to go to first grade, she was scared to death, knowing how "hard" it was going to be. She agreed with Margaret that she would go to class, but bring the work home to do. It took some time for Eileen to realize that the class was a breeze because she already knew the material.

Norman, who was a year younger than Eileen, simply absorbed everything around him. He wasn't challenged until he got to college and took architecture. Margaret didn't settle for school activities. She saw that after school the girls went to dance school with Mrs. Carter, at the Severna Park Y.W.C.A. Actually the dance class was a sort of fringe benefit that they got because Margaret started teaching at Anne Arundel Community College and was bringing home a paycheck. Dance class included ballet, tap, and acrobatics at each session. Eileen was in second grade, and Cindy was in fourth grade when they started. I remember the year-end recitals. They went on for many hours as each class put on a show dance for each of the types of dance, and each appearance was a different costume! The girls danced in the classes on up to their senior year in high school. Those lessons developed strong muscles and the recitals taught them to perform in front of audiences. Both were significant benefits.

Dancing wasn't enough. Along with that came music lessons. Cynthia started on flute with private lessons in 6th grade. She stayed with it up into high school. Eileen and Norman took piano lessons. The result was they could play together, duets. Being the same size and looks, people thought it was twins playing together. They were a stunning pair. The piano only lasted while they were in elementary school. In junior high, the top thing was Miss Harper's band. It was top notch. You had to audition and play well to get in. You also had to make all the rehearsals and be a faithful musician to practice. [Margaret adds: Which also meant mother had to drive to school each morning to deliver kids for band practice!]

Eileen picked oboe and really struggled despite private lessons. The instrument is one of the most difficult instruments and requires a professionally crafted reed. The purchased reeds were expensive and always seemed to be too hard or too soft. There weren't many other oboe players and by high school, I think, she was the only one. Norman made a better choice in the saxophone. He picked that up rapidly after piano as he could read music.

They all played in Miss Harper's band for three years—that's 7th, 8th, and 9th grades. It was a rewarding experience because the band was such high caliber. For several of those years, the Annapolis Junior High was on double sessions—too many students. I need to mention that the Mayo Elementary at that time brought in many portable classrooms as the school was too small. Eileen and Norman were both in one of those temporary portable rooms. Also at that time, I was the PTA President, and was frustrated over conditions. We simply had to put up with the mushrooming population and lack of facilities.

The junior high, during the time that Eileen and Norman attended, had one session from about 8 am until noon. Then the second session with all new students and new teachers was held in the afternoon. Miss Harper's band met at noon between the two school sessions. Of course she had the musicians from both sessions. Our children were always on the morning session. The school had a strict rule that no food was allowed during school hours. Miss Harper maintained that rule too, so Norman and Eileen couldn't eat from six o'clock breakfast until they returned home on the school bus about 2 in the afternoon. It was really tough. Norman fixed his own lunch of a can of Campbell's chunky soup each afternoon. He learned to love chunky soup.

Coming from a top-notch band, the girls had a big letdown when they reached the Southern High School band in the town of Harwood. Harwood was about 10 miles south of us in what we call "South County." The band at Southern was so poor that both girls dropped out, Cynthia after two years and Eileen during the first year. Poor Eileen was the only oboe, instead of having strong support in the oboe section.

Naturally the children took school busses to all their schools. Margaret got them up in the dark to catch that terribly early junior high bus. It was much earlier than the elementary or high school bus. I don't think that I participated. The good news was that the county was building new schools. Central High, later named South River High, was built on Central Avenue in Mayo, just a little, one mile, east of Loch Haven.

Next to the high school, they built a new junior high, and down a bit farther, a new elementary school for special students. These new schools were not completed soon enough for the girls, but Norman, after a year of half day school at Annapolis Junior High, got into the first class at Central Middle. His was the first graduating class of that school and of South River High. At least the band was better in the high school and he continued with his saxophone, adding flute and clarinet. And he was able to play saxophone in college in the various bands.

[Margaret recalls: There is an interesting sidelight to the construction of the schools. The county owned land off of Loch Haven Drive—it's now a county park. The county had retained the land in expectation of using it for schools. When the new schools were in the planning stage, we were thinking our children would be able to walk to elementary school! What a joy that would be! However, the black school children would be bussed in and their local school would be closed in favor of the larger integrated school. The black community protested. They petitioned that the location was unfair because their children would be bussed, but white children could walk, making extracurricular events more accessible to the white children. The school plans were delayed, and then scrapped in favor of the Central Avenue location, which meant that virtually ALL the children had to be bussed. The black school was turned into a community center, which was what the black population really wanted anyway. That's politics, folks!]

We were sorry that the girls missed out and went so far away to a weaker high school in South County. In particular, the girls took chemistry from an incompetent teacher. That teacher spent so much time on trivial procedures that she never taught most of the subject. Most of the textbook was left untouched. In college, Cynthia took chemistry again, and actually suffered because she had no background! Teachers really do make the difference in the quality of the school program. Southern High has made good progress, because they are now rated "Blue Ribbon"—a high-quality school.

Norman had a good high school. South River High was all new— new classrooms, new teachers and new administration. He took advanced courses like calculus and played his saxophone in both bands, the pep band, and the concert band. He also got to play a solo in the individual competition performances held at the U. of MD. At the request of the band teacher, he even took up a second instrument and played a bit of flute. There were no AP courses at that time, though there were easy classes and college prep classes. Norman was able to take college prep classes. He graduated with high honors in that first class from South River High.

Summers were always a big time for us. On the odd years we were home in Loch Haven. That meant swimming practically every day at our community beach. The children all joined the local swim team, which practiced at the Loch Haven beach. They swam competitions from about 5 years old on up to 10. The children were good at whatever they did and it didn't matter to us who won the individual races. They were ok to compete. They seldom won a race, but often placed. They dropped out of the community team at the 12 and under level because they didn't get to practice on the years that we drove to visit grandparents, and they were falling behind in skill, and in size. The Bigger kids (yes, that was really their last name) were just taller than our late bloomers.

They also took the Red Cross swimming lessons, which were offered free, at the beach. They advanced to junior lifesaving lessons, and after that they got to take lifesaving at the beach. Eileen managed also to take most of the Water Safety Instructor course in Annapolis at Truxton Park, although she completed the course at University of West Virginia. Cynthia completed Water Safety Instructor at Western Maryland College and she later taught swim classes at the Loch Haven beach. By then the Red Cross had ceased sponsoring the swim classes, so they were privately sponsored by the Loch Haven Civic Association.

At the Community beach, I enjoyed throwing each one up into the air so they could dive back in the water. We also dived off of the anchored platform out in the deeper water—about 6 feet deep. Our Civic Association put up a sea nettle net around the platform and beach area. Small nettles could get under the net, so I spent a lot of time picking them up and throwing them up on the beach to dry out. A nettle is well over 90% water and so nothing is left after they dry out. The nettles like salt water. That means on dry years, when the bay water is salty, the nettles are thick. On a real wet year, the nettles are sparse and come in late, not until August.

In addition, the children went fishing with me in one of my boats. The first thing I bought [Margaret exclaims: before we bought furniture!] was an aluminum hull, 14-foot long boat with a 7-½ horsepower outboard engine. It was only good in South River. I remember taking my mother, Pearl, out while she held little Cynthia, maybe 2, and the wind came up. Mom was scared that we wouldn't make it back as the spray came up in our faces.

After a few years, I got a 16-foot runabout with a 40 horsepower outboard. That boat would make it down to the mouth of South River and out to Thomas Point Light where I liked to fish. I caught small rockfish then at the point. The limit was only 12 inches at the time. The first sturdy boat that I bought new was an 18-foot tri-hull with an inboard motor. That was a big step up as the inboard was a regular GM block, as in a car, and adapted to water with an outdrive down the back of the hull. It was about 150 horsepower and strong enough to pull skiers. Of course, we all took up waterskiing. As we practiced in Brewer Creek, in calm water, we presented an amusing sight to our waterfront neighbors. They watched us get up and fall down over and over.

We all got good at jumping the waves behind the boat. Normally, it was one child at a time, but we had a rig for two. The girls would ski in a pair, trying to cross over behind the boat. The bad time was when Cynthia got one leg tangled in Eileen's rope and was pulled through the water until I stopped the boat. Cynthia got a bad rope burn on her lower leg that required a skin graft. She still has the scar today. The burn put her on crutches on the first few days of high school in September. Fortunately some of her friends helped her up and down the school stairs and carried her books from class to class. Needless to say, we went back to one skier at a time. We contrived to ski on up through the children's high school years. I skied right along with them all those years and got quite good at it.

Next, I bought a small cabin cruiser with a red hull and maybe a 225 horsepower engine. That boat lasted me some 14 years from 1986 to 2000. It had a nice cabin with bunks. We did sleep in the boat on a trip to St. Michael's over on the Eastern shore. Margaret and I went to the museum, saw the sights, and slept overnight in the harbor. My last and current boat is a "Sea Sport," almost 26 feet long, with a 250 horsepower inboard. It is a fishing boat, small cabin with a big open back for fishing. It is equipped with rod holders, bait wells, fish boxes, and all appropriate equipment. Margaret doesn't care to sleep in the boat, so I only take day trips, usually fishing in the Bay, and coming home early. The fishing has gotten real poor in recent years, as pollution has gone up and water quality down. I still catch some bottom fish: white perch, croaker, and Norfolk spot in the summer, and maybe a few rock fish in fall. The limit is now 18 inches on the rock fish.

The even years were even more adventuresome, as we took cross-country trips. We learned an awful lot about camping over those years. Perhaps the first year was a significant lesson. We had our tent and sleeping bags in an open rack above the station wagon, a Ford wagon. On day one, we were heading toward my cousin's house, Bettie Anne Logan, in Knoxville, Tennessee. Well, it rained cats and dogs on the way. A hurricane was passing by. We stopped at Luray Caverns as a diversion and had an almost private tour as no one else braved the storm. Then, when we stopped for gas on the freeway, the ladies' room was flooded. The attendant at the gas station was saying that he couldn't leave because the local roads were flooded. Everything got wet, even the sleeping bags under the tarp on top of the station wagon. But we stopped at a camp ground and had to get through the night. Margaret and I slept in the back of the wagon on a foam pad, with a light blanket, and the three ka-boopers were in the small tent, huddled under the one dry sleeping bag. From there, we drove little country roads to the Logan's house and stayed a few days with them before heading west. The sleeping bags dried out on their clothesline out back of their house.

I particularly recall the "chiggers." We normally pulled into campsites where all the good places were reserved for trailers with "hook ups." We would end up at a tent site out on the periphery, maybe in the grass. AT one of the first sites in Eastern Arkansas, we got eaten, full of chigger bites. Our trips would take us due west from Arkansas to Oklahoma, across the panhandle of West Texas, through New Mexico, to Tucson, Arizona. In general, the camping was good west of the Mississippi River, because you could count on dry weather. We generally gave up camping east of the Mississippi. In fact, the first couple of times across country, when the children were real small, we stayed in cheap motels. The great adventures were the camping trips in the late 60's and through the 70's.

[Margaret adds: I remember one night in one of those motels. We stopped at a place that had laundry facilities, so I collected clothes to wash. While they were washing, Carvel and I and Cindy walked around a little. Norman was tucked into a motel crib. Eileen, age three or so, was sleeping in the room. But she woke up, and amused herself with the little chain on the door. She managed to put the chain in the slot that prevents the door from opening. When we returned and tried to get in—well, the door wouldn't open all the way. When we opened it to talk to her and tell her how to unchain the door, the chain was taut and she couldn't move it. When we closed the door, she didn't know what to do to unlock it. We panicked. There was no other way into the room. The motel manager came out to see the problem, and he was stumped too. But he noticed our scruffy appearance. Eventually, to our relief, Eileen managed to undo the chain and let us in. Then I discovered that the dryer in the motel didn't work well. I spread damp laundry out all over the interior of the room. The next morning the manager showed up to "help us" with our luggage. But I think that he believed we were making off with his sheets and towels—or were likely to. We just had a general mess in the room.]

Returning to camping—in Oklahoma, a number of times, we camped near a beautiful large lake. Over in Texas we went to the annual outdoor musical show in Red Rock Canyon and saw the depiction of the history of Texas, followed by a live fire fall down the sheer cliff across from the amphitheatre. In New Mexico, we stopped at the "bottomless" lakes part, even went swimming. The lakes were called bottomless because the early settlers measured the depth of a lake by dropping a rope down. These lakes funneled into a deep river, so the settlers' rope never reached a bottom. One time when we were there, the camping supervisors didn't want us to swim because a week before a man had been in a rowboat in the center of the lake and had just stepped out and gone down like a rock. The management had had to bring in deep-sea divers to haul his body up. We were unafraid of the deep water, and we detested the "Olympic sized" swimming pool there because it was only 3 feet deep! We swam in the lake, regardless. The ranger eyed us a while to check that we could indeed swim.

In Tucson, Arizona, we stayed with my parents for weeks, maybe a month. In later years, as the children grew, my parents rented a motel with a pool so we had extra activity. Mom did all our meals, 3 a day, at home, and she truly enjoyed the cooking. All of us enjoyed picking the lemons off the lemon tree and especially the huge grapefruit off that tree. Dad saved some of the grapefruit all winter long so we could pick them in June. What a feast. Mom counted the grapefruit all year as they were picked and ran her count up to the 1000's, all on one tree! We also picked grapes off the trellis beside the carport and watched the flowers bloom. There were oleanders across the back yard, my father's big wooden bucket of gardenias, and the cacti: barrel, sequoia, prickly pear and others all bloomed. It was just a big family reunion every time we got to Tucson.

On those years that we drove out, 60's and 70's, we continued on from Tucson to San Marino, California, to visit the Owens. Belva, Margaret's Mom, died from cancer, melanoma, in 1964, so from then on it was a visit to Dr. Owens and Margaret's sister, Elizabeth.

One summer I signed up for a continuing ed course in computers at UCLA—computers were a very new thing in 1964—where I learned programming. Every weekend meant a commute back to San Marino and the family.

One summer we drove directly to California first. That trip took us across the middle states: Missouri, Kansas, and Nevada into the backside of the California mountains. We visited some relatives of Margaret in St. Louis and of course saw the great arch. We all remember Kansas as flat and on forever. We drove all day long one day in Kansas and were still in Kansas. That trip brought us across the desert, dry lands of Nevada, to the Sierra Mountains, just east of Yosemite Park in California. It was mid-June, and at the base of the mountains we found out the back road up had just been cleared of snow that weekend! How fortunate. We made it up and over driving between plowed snow some 10 feet high on each side of the road. Are you amazed at how the innocent or rather the "dumb" get by! We had reservations at Yosemite for a cabin, and if we'd missed our date we'd be out of luck. As it was, we pulled in to check in just about at closing time. Margaret made the reservations over 6 months ahead because the cabins were booked solid for the summers.

We camped one night in Yosemite National Park and saw as much of the sights as we could. Spectacular was Yosemite Falls gushing with the spring melt some 2000 feet down various cliffs. We drove through the mammoth redwood tree that had been tunneled out with a road through it. The tree was still growing fine. It's long gone. Now, in fact, you can't camp or drive through the park anymore. I think you have to take a park bus now to get to the heart of the park. "Half Dome" was there like a huge sphere cut in half. I had already climbed to the top of Half Dome back when I was at U. of California, not too far away. The climb was up the back, or round side. Next we drove on to visit our folks, arriving well after midnight in San Marino, much to Dr. Owens' astonishment. He was sure that we must have stopped along the way at a motel.

The longest of our summer trips was a complete 9000-mile circuit around the country. After visiting in Tucson and San Marino, we headed north up the coastal highway through California and Oregon. There were wonderful views of the Pacific Ocean along the way. At the Columbia River, we headed inland along the water. There were lots of camp areas, but we kept going to make miles. Suddenly, there were NO campsites. We crossed the river on a bridge to get to a park in Washington. We were told by the manager, who was reluctant to let us stay at all, to pitch the tent 'way over to the side off the pavement and away from the other trailer campers. To our shock, at midnight the sprinklers came on and sprayed water into the children's tent and the parents' station wagon. Despite the heat, everyone closed up windows! Isn't it nice that our children would put up with anything!

After Washington state came Idaho, with the attraction of "craters of the Moon." The area was coated with porous volcanic magma. In the cooled magma were large craters or holes in the ground. They were deep and filled with ice at the bottom. I guess the ice never completely melted. It was a rare sight. We crossed the Snake River and on into Montana. The big attraction was Glacier National Park with the ice fields and glaciers. We planned to stay there 3 days. The children were delighted. For once they could leave the tent up and not pack it every morning. So much for plans! We camped near the Western Edge of the park because that area was the only one available. But most of the good hikes started from the Eastern side. So, the next morning we packed up and moved to the East to St. Mary's Campground. That night a huge wind arose and blew the tent down. Of course, Margaret and I are snug in the back of the station wagon. We moved the tent to the third site in the morning and drove to a hike across a glacier.

One unpleasant event involved the car. We drove to the glacier hike early in the morning with the car lights on, and I failed to turn the lights off in bright daylight. At the end of the day after hiking the glacier, we discovered our battery was dead. One Ford man, whose camper was next to our car, tried to jump-start us to no avail. He said that the battery was shot—killed by being run completely out. Well, somehow I got hold of a mechanic at a near service station. He knew something! First he put water, pure, into the battery and then charged it up. The battery took a full charge and was ok.

It was July and we were freezing there in Glacier National Park! We actually bought some sweatshirts to survive! That night the tent stayed up, but in the morning it was time to pack up and drive on. Then on East. That ended the children's big chance to not pack the tent. It was a different spot every night. The bottom line was we all had a good time.

We were driving not far from the Canadian border, across Montana and North Dakota, on south to South Dakota. We went out of our way, off the highway, to Devil's Tower. Most worthwhile, it was a very sharp peak, rising straight up from flat ground. Passing through the "Bad Lands," we came to Mt. Rushmore and viewed the great presidents' faces. It's a thrill to see Washington, Jefferson, and Lincoln looking at you from the top of the mountain. I would have liked to have stopped in Groton, South Dakota, my father's hometown, but we didn't have the time. By this time we were melting from the heat, despite being northerly.

On south we traveled through Minnesota, the twin cities St. Paul and Minneapolis, the city where I was born. Then we passed by the University of Wisconsin where both my parents graduated. Finally we came into Illinois and headed east. We found it best not to camp from Illinois on home—not dry enough.

The final leg took us across Indiana, Ohio, into Pennsylvania. We crossed Pennsylvania on the turnpike and finally south to home in Maryland. The good news is that we camped out essentially every night for two months while traveling a total of 9000 miles. That trip will be always in the memories of my family! A summer of summers!

Other summer trips were just as exciting, but not so long. We took in most of the great national parks. While in Tucson, Carvel's parents took us south to Nogales, Mexico, just to say we'd been there. Several times from Tucson we went to northern Arizona to see the Grand Canyon, and the Hoover Dam. I remember, along Lake Meade, we had to get out of the wagon overnight and sleep on a picnic table. It was so hot with radiation from the surrounding rocks. From there, we took a loop by the Valley of Fires, temperature in the valley reached 130 degrees F. My air conditioner would knock off maybe 30 degrees, so it was still 100 degrees in the car! We stopped at a ranger station and asked for car gas. They didn't have any and the closest station ahead was in Las Vegas, hours away. The station wagon needed frequent gas stops. It couldn't make it to Las Vegas, so I left Margaret and the kids in the cool ranger station and drove back to a marina on Lake Meade, bought a couple of gallons of boat gas off a pier into a can. That gas got us into town across the desert. We were so happy to get from there to Las Vegas.

On other occasions in our bi-yearly cross country trips we went north from Arizona into Utah. Zion Park in Utah was a major stop. We camped along the river and took the narrows hike up the river, walking in the water. After a few miles of river walking, we got to where the canyon walls were almost arms' length apart. At one place near camp, the 3 children hiked up to the rim of the canyon on a narrow trail. Margaret and I watched from below.

From Zion, we traveled on up to Bryce Canyon for more terrific hikes. Bryce has been sculpted, mostly by wind, into unbelievable pillars, arches, and all imaginable shapes. It is a wonderland of nature. We also drove up Pike's Peak while the road was still open to the top.

We passed through Salt Lake City on the Great Salt Lake and had a tour of the Mormon Temple. That is something you must see. We even took a dip in the salt water. On to the North, you run into Wyoming and the great Yellowstone National Park. In those days it wasn't quite as crowded as it is now, and you could get reasonably close to the natural wonders. Old Faithful was roped off, but we walked up to the mud pots and hot springs to see the brilliant colors. Strong chemicals bubbled up in the water to color the rocks and sand, even mud. We saw several other geysers erupt besides Old Faithful. We drove on though to the mountains and saw the Tetons. Almost everywhere in the West are impressive mountains. For us Easterners, all these mountains made an everlasting imprint. Ask my children what they got from summer trips!

Just a final note. As we traveled, the children would say, "Don't let Momma look!" as we passed a sign for a museum or a nearby attraction. They knew it was a stop before we could pass on! We went through the dinosaur museums, the Indian museums, the Wild West museums, and whatever came up along the routes. In particular, we saw the Buffalo Bill show in Laramie, Wyoming with the roping, the wild bucking rides, the whole cultural tradition of the wild west. I think we well covered the National Parks and scenic attractions of the good old U.S. of A. Our country is second to none in beautiful vistas. All of this sightseeing is worthy of your time and a valuable picture to carry in hour heart.

Family, Carvel, Margaret, Cynthia, Norman standing,
Eileen next to Margaret, about 1968

CHAPTER 10

Continuing at the Naval Academy

All those years along with sweet Margaret raising three dynamic children, I continued teaching the midshipmen. They were mostly good students and a pleasure to teach. My teaching subjects expanded to include Probability and Statistics, and Advanced Engineering Mathematics, including Partial Differential Equations. Computers and time-sharing on our main frame giant, a Honeywell, became standard in all classes and offices. We had to time share because the computer, with vacuum tubes and wires, occupied a compete room for one Honeywell computer, but there were a number of outlets and the computer switched back and forth from user to user. We taught the students programming and had them solve tough math problems on the computer. It was all new to me, as the computer didn't exist when I was a budding student. I learned everything on the job!

In particular, I specialized in the subject of Linear Programming. That had a unique technique called "The Simplex Method," which optimized an objective function subject to many linear constraints. It required repeated iterations, called pivots, that could require millions of cycles around a loop. Naturally, the problems could only be done on a high-speed computer.

I wrote the programs in the "True Basic" language, which carried out the entire process to the final maximum or minimum solution. For example, you might be maximizing a profit, or perhaps minimizing a cost in a business situation. Popular, were transportation problems to minimize the cost involved.

Since I made up the course, the problems, and the programming, I decided to publish the text. My first text came out in 1973. It was titled "Linear Programming with Fortran," Actually the text contained all the programs in both the Fortran and the True Basic languages. Fortran was the first popular computer language, and then True Basic was developed at Dartmouth to simplify the process. I really liked the True Basic language! The book was published by Scott Foresman, and was used at the Naval Academy until 1985. I became "Mr. Linear Program," in our math department. It was my privilege to teach the elective course to seniors, mostly math majors, all those years using my own book.

Much more difficult and challenging was the companion subject of "Integer Programming." The difference from linear programming was that the answers were required to be integers (Margaret notes: for us ordinary folks, that means whole numbers), instead of general fractions or decimals. If you were selling objects, you naturally had to sell a whole number of the products to each customer. So integer programming became the industry standard for businesses.

The mathematics involved was all brand new math techniques called "cutting planes," and "branch and bound." Again, I wrote the computer programs for the new techniques and then published a second book in 1985. The new version included both linear and integer programming. It also took up the latest methods and their programs. The book, published by Prentice-Hall, came with a computer disc that included five of the needed programs to do each type of problem. I taught the course using my new book until the subject was dropped around 1990. The ideas of linear and integer programming got incorporated in a broader course called Operations Analysis. Actual programming by then was unnecessary as the appropriate techniques were all on the large computers.

Today the techniques are all commercialized and stored in the big computers so no one had to do the thinking—just follow instructions for setting up the problem as given by the computer. The day of individual programming is over! Today, we just formulate the problems and then turn the data over to the computer to find the solution.

In my early days at the math department we had a softball team that played the other departments. Of course, I played on our team, some infield, but mostly outfield. My best position was hitter, as I usually got on base. One time I slid into home plate in a very close play, and the catcher came down on my chest with both knees. Well, I'm sure he either broke or tore loose a lower rib. For umpteen months I had a floating rib.

Our other main activity was the bowling league. Each department in the "yard" fielded a team, for about a10 team league. We bowled once a week, first at the lanes in the Naval Station across the Severn River, and then on the lanes put in at the basement of Bancroft Hall. Bancroft Hall was the dormitory that housed all 4000 midshipmen. They had their bowling on some other day or evening.

The result is, I have a whole chest full of trophies from team awards to individual awards. My best year I had the high average of some 176. A number of times our team won the league championship and received a piece of sliver—a tray or a bowl. I also got a high game award and a triplicate award for three games of exactly the same score. I enjoyed the bowling the entire 36 years of service at the Naval Academy. Also I continued to swim at lunch for the 36 years. I believe that swimming is the main reason for my good health all these years.

For many years our department bridge club met once a month for dessert and cards. When we joined, it drew three tables of players. The group gave out as fewer and fewer bridge players came into our department. Old habits seem to fade away in the new world. One more activity was our spring cookout. Several departments got together for a big feed and hamburger cookout with perhaps volleyball. The party was held along the Severn River Park at the Naval Station across the river from the Academy.

Professionally, I continued to work and write some papers in my field of linear and integer programming. One summer I attended a special class at American University in Washington, D.C. It was taught by the top authority in the field of logic, who was working for the U.S. government at the time. It was a real pleasure to listen and be stimulated. Another summer, while visiting the Owens family in San Marino, I took a computer course at UCLA where I wrote a program that found the roots of any polynomial. The nth-degree polynomial has n-roots. I stayed at a dorm on campus during the week and then enjoyed weekends at the Owens' home with the rest of my family. San Marino was across town from the UCLA campus. Margaret and family stayed with her father and Elizabeth for those six weeks. Margaret's mother had just died so Dick was rather alone.

We really enjoyed our cross country drives to my parents in Tucson, Arizona and Margaret's parents in a suburb of Los Angeles. We made the trip every other year, camping along the way.

Also, during these years, we became closer to my Uncle Seth and Aunt Melva in Baltimore. Their daughter, Kay, was close in age to Carvel and married about the same time. They had a daughter Kathy who was only a year older than our oldest, Cynthia. It began in 1962 with an invitation for Kay to bring Kathy to Cynthia's fourth birthday party, a small family affair. Then, because Kay was eager for Kathy to take swimming lessons, Kathy was invited for the week of swimming lessons at the Loch Haven beach. I was teaching at Johns Hopkins at night in the summer, so Kay brought Kathy over to the parking lot at Johns Hopkins to climb into my car for the drive to our house. A later week, Cynthia took the ride to Baltimore for a week with her city cousins. The girls got along just fine, so this summer exchange continued until they became teenagers. We tried the exchange with Kathy's younger son Rick and our Norman, but the boys didn't seem to hit it off so well.

Along about this time, Melva Wolfe realized that we were living close by but had no other relatives close by and she invited us to Thanksgiving dinner. It became a regular tradition. Thanksgiving morning Cynthia, Eileen, and Norman would sit at the dining room table and cut and peel apples from the tree in our side yard. Margaret would work through the directions on a box of pie crust mix, preparing pie crusts. Then the apples, spices and crust were combined and baked into several pies. The pies and family loaded into the car and I drove to Melva and Seth's house. The gathering always included the five of us, Seth and Melva, of course, and Kay and Dick Barrans and their two children, Kathy and Rick. Sometimes some others were there, and after serving in Vietnam, Seth junior, Melva's son, and his wife Charity and Seth's daughter Julie were there. Cynthia and Eileen thought the name Julie was such a pretty name that they named their dolls after her. It was a wonderful gathering.

I attended many meetings of our professional math organizations, the MAA (Mathematical Association of America) and the AMS (American Mathematical Society). Of course I was a member of both groups. At some meetings I presented papers or talks of my own work. I remember speaking in Virginia, and also here at the Academy. We also had some talk seminars here in our own department. The farthest I went to a professional meeting was to New Orleans, several times, where I enjoyed the cooking—especially a meal of red snapper covered with small shrimp. On another occasion, I stayed at Atlanta, GA, in a hotel with Margaret. The unusual event was the snowfall. The city couldn't handle it—no plows or equipment. The fire engine station, across from our building, we could see out our hotel window. The firemen were out shoveling with small coal shovels. I thought it was a riot! At least we were comfortable in the hotel, and the management managed to recruit enough workers to put on the scheduled banquet. Days later we made it to the airport, which had just opened, and flew home.

In 1980, I decided to go again for the PhD. It was required for a promotion to full professor. I found Walden University that had a summer program followed by a supervised time to write a thesis. That summer I went to their program on a campus in Kennebunkport Maine. All of the courses were completed plus a number of papers in the latest changes in your field. I particularly recall the steamed lobster we ate just off campus. That was a treat.

Back at the Academy, I took a sabbatical leave for six months that fall. That gave me full time every day to work on the computer and solve a set of scheduling problems that required integer programming. My supervisor was Professor Charles Mylander, right there in our department. It was most convenient. I actually published, in a professional journal, a paper on the conclusions of my work. The final work took me almost three years as I was back to teaching the semester after the sabbatical. The final version was submitted and approved by a professor in the field who lived up in Canada. I did actually get the PhD that summer 1983, at the Walden U graduation. The graduation was held at the U. of Minnesota in Saint Paul, Minnesota. I got my PhD hood, robe, and cap that I wore to all the following graduations at the Naval Academy stadium.

The final note on my career is a sad one. I fully expected a promotion after earning the PhD. My approval was ok with the head of our math department. Professor Archangelo gave me his ok, and spoke for me at the hearing before the yard-wide committee. That yard committee from all of the other departments voted me down and said that I had to publish more papers. Those "bull" professors published papers by the dozen and apparently one "good" paper was not enough. I was absolutely crushed. I put in for retirement as of January 1992, because I refused to teach any longer at a lower rank! If they had given me the promotion to full professor, I would have stayed on the faculty more years. So, my career ended and I went into retirement at age 64, in 1992. You may see that even the most fulfilling career and golden life, called abundant life, has some shortcomings.

CHAPTER 11

Children and Grandchildren

All of my children, two daughters and a son, graduated from college by the time I retired from the Naval Academy. Daughter Cynthia, the oldest, graduated from Western Maryland College in Westminster, MD. She majored in biology, but afterwards took graduate work in education so that she could teach. Her graduation was in June 1980 and shortly thereafter she married Greg Behm. Greg graduated from the same school two years earlier and then got his master's degree in business administration that year. The big wedding in July 1980 was held at our church, Mayo United Methodist Church. Of course, it was a beautiful wedding with all the trimmings. I particularly remember the great trumpet solo. A friend of Greg was a superb player and volunteered his solo before going to join the St. Louis symphony orchestra. Cynthia taught for a while as Greg worked first with Scott Paper, and then with Marriott hotels.

Their first son, and our first grandson, was born on 4 July 1984. David has always had the distinction of celebrating his birthday on the Independence Day of our country. Cynthia continued to bless us with more sons. Our second grandson, Brian, was born on 3 December, 1985, and the third grandson was born on 6 April 1988. We have been very close to the whole family, partly because they settled in Maryland, up near Westminster.

Our second daughter, Eileen, attended West Virginia University, in Morgantown, West Virginia for two years. She then transferred to St. Louis University in St. Louis, MO. The transfer was important as she was majoring in Physical Therapy. The program at West Virginia was limited, mostly, to in-state students, but actually, the physical therapy program in St. Louis was one of the best in the country. She really studied hard at West Virginia when she realized that she needed those high grades to get into the program. Also, she put in over a 100 hours of volunteering at the West Virginia Hospital. In addition, she worked summers at a camp for the handicapped in Anne Arundel County. She was highly motivated and experienced all along the way.

Eileen worked at her profession, physical therapy, for several years before marriage. She bragged that she was our only child who had to seek, apply for, and find a job right after graduation. Cynthia got married right away, and son Norman went directly into military service after his graduation.

Eileen married Jim Thibodeau, whom she met while he held a job as industrial engineer at Westinghouse in northern Anne Arundel County. At the time, Eileen was working as a physical therapist in county schools and had her own apartment. Jim also lived in one of the near-by apartments. They were likewise married in our United Methodist church in 1984. Jim was unhappy in the job and decided to return to school. He went back to college to get some business education and to seek a new field at a college in Florida, but took a temporary job as industrial engineer in Jacksonville. While in Jacksonville, FL, Eileen worked at Nemours Hospital for Children. Unhappy in his job, Jim decided on a new career in optometry—a dramatic change from engineer. To make the change, Jim and Eileen moved to Houston, TX where he earned his degree in Optometry. The good news was that wherever they went, Eileen was in demand and got a job right off. She mostly covered their expenses in Texas until her first son came along on 15 Dec 1989. His name was Kevin. He was very precocious from early on. He caught on to everything very early. Because he was an early riser and an active tot, he became an expert on the computer and especially computer games. Before he was five, he actually taught himself how to play chess by experimenting with the chess game on the computer before breakfast each morning.

In the summer of 1991, Kevin and Eileen visited us at our home in Loch Haven while she suffered through a second pregnancy. I remember Kevin standing on a stool at our bathroom window looking out at a work crew that was digging a new septic well for us. His attention span would last an hour or more, and he was less than two years old! Jim was back in Texas, working on his degree. But Eileen stayed with us so long that summer that the friends in church began to believe that she and Jim had split up!

While Jim and Eileen were still in Texas, their second son, Jason, was born on 10 October 1991. Jason was shy and different from Kevin, but still very smart. Shortly after his birth Jim graduated and they moved to Lakeland, FL. They lived in town near First Methodist church and could walk to preschool there. They could also walk, later to their elementary school. Both boys got all A's in school. They also played soccer locally and in school.

Eileen's daughter, Karen, came along 7 June 1994, and was our ninth grandchild. (Norman's kids sneaked in there.) She completed our family with a total of 7 grandsons and 2 granddaughters. Karen is also an A student in school and a real beauty. At the age of 15, she entered a contest in Seventeen Magazine sponsored by a hair product, and, with the help of her brothers and extended family and friends on the computer voting, came out the winner. She and her mother were flown to California for a professional photo shoot and later that year she had a full page spread in the Seventeen magazine. I still have that magazine with her gorgeous pictures, a real beauty. She also did some cheerleading and some running at school. Of course we are very proud of her and all 9 grandchildren.

By the way, Jim did become an optometrist, and located his practice in Lakeland, FL. For professional reasons and others, he changed the family name from Thibodeau to Summers. The family has grown up in Florida and every year, mostly in the spring we have visited Florida. It was a nice exchange for us to spend a week on the Gulf Coast beach and also visit the Summers.

Now, look at our third child and son, Norman, born 9 September 1961. He was only 15 months younger than Eileen and soon grew to her size. As small children they played together and were judged, on first glance by others, to be twins. They looked somewhat alike and were continually enjoying the same activity. In late elementary school the two of them took piano lessons, and at one of the recitals, they played a duet on the one piano. Later, by junior high school, Norman played saxophone and Eileen played the oboe in Miss Harper's famous Annapolis

Junior High Band. Cynthia played flute in the Harper band when she was attending Annapolis Junior High. That gave each one three years of good band experience. The two girls dropped out of the Southern High Band because it was so poor in comparison. Norman, however, went to the brand new Central High School (now South River High School) and continued in the band even into college. Norman had the distinction of being in the first graduating class of Central. He also graduated near the top of his class.

Norman won a ROTC scholarship at the U. of Virginia, so that he got officer's training along with school. He chose to major in architecture mostly, we think, because it was a challenge. All the other subjects were too easy! He continued to play sax in the college marching band and pep band. Upon graduation, 1983, he was commissioned a second lieutenant in the army. His army career lasted about 10 years, with the initial years of deployment in Germany. We got to visit him twice on trips to Germany in 1985 and again in 1987. On the 1985 visit, we took a wonderful sightseeing excursion to Greece. The summer of 1987 included a tour of Denmark, Sweden, Norway and Finland. Norman married an army nurse, Nancy Paetow, in 1985. The wedding was held on Long Island, New York, near Nancy's parents' home. They both served in Germany the first two years of their marriage. Their first child, Cara, was born when they just had returned from Germany on 5 December 1987. Cara was small and had trouble gaining weight her initial year. She did grow and become a healthy active and smart girl in school.

In the states again, Norman was stationed at a facility near the Pentagon that designed and maintained medical facilities for the army. He actually got to use some of his architectural ability. The family lived in Manassas, VA where son Mark was born on 10 May 1989. Mark really grew tall, and is now, at 22, taller than I. The family moved again to Denver, Colorado, where Norman served his last army assignment at the Veteran's Hospital. That's where he got into hospital administration. Norman was a rank Captain now, and was looking for promotion. However, the promotion did not come through, and on the usual up or out basis, he dropped the army. He returned to college in Denver, where he received a double master's degree in Business and Hospital administration. Norman and Nancy's last child, Ryan, was born in

Denver on 21 April 1992. Norman got a job managing the medical facilities in Antarctica and went a number of times to McMurdo station and to the South Pole. He saw that the stations got their needed medical equipment and that the personnel had satisfied medical examiners before they left the states. There was no in or out at the pole during the winter months, so all transported people and supplies had to be coordinated for movement during the Antarctic summer months.

The whole family became avid skiers and very good. Mark, in particular became expert on the snowboard, his favorite. Ryan developed into a great skier, like his father, Norman. The two of them did all the most difficult double black diamond slopes, in particular, the big moguls (bumps).

It is interesting to see how our interest in skiing passed on to the grandchildren. When David Behm, the oldest, was just finished first grade, we took him to Hidden Valley resort in Pennsylvania and introduced him to skis. Actually, we hired ski lessons at the resort. I led him down one of the hills after his lessons. He caught on like a natural. We did the same thing with his younger brother Brian at age 6—introduced him to skiing. When Gary, the youngest, came along, he got to experience skiing at an earlier age—before school—because the Behm parents became interested and we all went skiing as an extended family.

Getting such an early start, they all became expert skiers as teenagers. Brian, in particular liked jumps. He took off from any bump in the trail and then later did the jumps on the terrain park. Gary got a semester of college in Utah to learn back country ski and rescue techniques. Then, his first summer after college, Gary took a summer job in Alaska, which required him to learn special guide and rescue methods up on the local glaciers.

All three of Cynthia and Greg's boys graduated from college. David graduated from Bridgeport College in Stanton, VA, with a degree in Business Administration. He worked at a bank in Baltimore, MD for close to two years and then moved to Denver CO. In Colorado he worked first at a small ski rental shop in Breckenridge, and then for a leading sporting goods company in Denver, and is now (2011) learning management with that company.

Brian and Gary both graduated from Messiah College in PA. Brian was an art major, on a merit scholarship, and specialized in commercial (graphic) art. Jobs were very scarce when he graduated, so Brian worked at Starbucks, brewing and serving coffee for a couple of years. He now has a professional job in commercial art in Baltimore, MD. Brian married Victoria in August 2110. They are (2011) living in an apartment in Baltimore where they both work. She also graduated from Messiah College.

As I write, Gary is set to marry Claire in September 2011. That will be the second wedding of the grandchildren. Business administration was also Gary's major, and he is working at R.E.I., a large sporting goods store in Baltimore. He also expects to move into management. Claire is a nurse and is working at Johns Hopkins Hospital.

Going back to Norman and Nancy Wolfe's children, Cara graduated from University of Washington in Seattle with a major in orthotics. She was always interested in making braces and working with children in need. For several summers in high school and college, she had shadowed a friend of her mother who worked in that field. Now, she is doing a graduate internship at Duke University in North Carolina. By the way she is also an expert skier. Norman saw that his children all got into skiing. We all ski together each season when Margaret and I go to Colorado every winter.

Mark, Norman's first son, graduated from a junior college in Colorado. Again, there were no jobs. Mark went to an industrial school in Denver this year, 2010-2011, and learned both heating and air conditioning repair and maintenance. After months of looking, he finally found a job in heating and air conditioning the summer of 2011. By the way, he naturally learned to ski, but switched over to the snowboard. So, he boards with us, as we all go skiing.

Finally, Ryan, the younger son, graduated from high school in June 2010. As I already mentioned he became a great skier and worked at a local pool as swimming instructor and lifeguard. He climbed mountains with Dad, Norman, and "collected" the 14'ers—the local Colorado mountains over 14,000 feet. He planned to climb a new one each year of his young life. He was interested in becoming a pilot and was signed up to attend a college in North Dakota, which included a flying program. The saddest of events is that Ryan died of some heart condition in July 2010. Nobody has been able to explain the why's or the how's. Everyone thought that he was in perfect health, as a most active teenager. He actually died the night before a scheduled flight to Maryland to visit us at our home. What a blow!

Now, to wrap up the positions of Eileen and Jim Summer's three children in Florida. Kevin is at the Florida State University with one year to go. He is following mother Eileen, in taking physical therapy, but he may yet change his direction. He is engaged to Alise Huff, and they plan to wed May of 2012, when they both graduate from college. Brother Jason is in his sophomore year and has a pre-med declared major. His University is in Orlando Florida, where he stays on campus. Finally, Karen, our last grandchild is still in high school, but a senior. She is a beautiful young lady, and very talented. She expects to graduate in June 2012 with flying colors and all A's, another top student. Her graduation is close to the same time that Kevin is graduating from the University. My how time flies and how fast all the grandchildren have grown up!

Gary Behm and Claire did have a magnificent wedding in September of 2011. The dinner for the wedding rehearsal was held at my house in Loch Haven right on South River. The wedding, on Sunday, was held at Mayo Beach outdoors next to South River. Another party and dinner shortly after the ceremony was right there in the large Mayo pavilion, a county maintained park. They are the second couple living and working in Baltimore along with Brian Behm and Victoria.

Of course, things move on, I was still writing on through 2012. Karen Summers did graduate from high school and is attending the same university in Florida as her brother Jason. He, Jason, is taking pre-med and will probably go on to med school. Kevin Summers graduated from Florida State U. and married Alise. He is now in a medical college in South Carolina studying to be a doctor.

Back to the Behm's, David married Tirza, a physical therapist, out in Denver in 2012 and they are both working locally. Gary and Claire also moved out to Denver where she works as a nurse and he has a business position. Brian and Victoria remain in Baltimore, both working. So all three Behm grandchildren are settled as working families.

The remaining Wolfe grandchildren, Norman and Nancy's children, are still single with Mark working in Denver. Mark veries from living in an apartment to living back at home. Cara Wolfe finished her career training in orthotics and is now a certified full time worker in Durham, North Carolina. I will close my writing on them here as a most proud Grandpa.

Carvel & Margaret with grandchildren, Daved, Brian, Gary Behm;
Kevin, Jason, Karen Summers; Cara, Mark, Ryan Wolfe, 2008

Lunar Eclipse!
(This piece was written the day it happened!)

Today, 21 December of 2010, is a day I will remember. First of all was the night rest, that for me was exceptional. I turned in early, being tired, at 9:30 PM. When I awoke it was 3:30 AM, a sleep of six hours. In recent years, my sleep has been irregular, usually only 2 or 3, maybe 4, hours at a stretch. I would wake up and get up briefly through the night. Anyway, the 21st of December was the winter solstice, that is, the longest night and the shortest day of the year. In addition there was a complete eclipse of the moon that night. The last time these two events occurred together was way back in the 16 hundreds.

The total eclipse of the moon, a passing of the moon through the shadow of the earth, lasted from 2:41 AM until after 5 AM. My awakening at 3:30 AM was conveniently during the middle of totality. So I got up, put on a warm hat, coat, gloves, right over my PJ's and went out into the subfreezing night. To get a good view, away from the trees, I walked up to the road.

The moon was spectacular. It was brown—sort of an orange shade of brown. I was amazed you could see the moon in shadow, not reflecting any sun rays. However, there was apparently some reflection from the atmosphere. The color was determined by the amount and kind of particles in our air: namely our air pollution. The color was predicted to be anywhere from brown to red. The reality was a light brown! So, I saw my first total eclipse of the moon—and on a solstice night!

CHAPTER 12

Early Retirement

First I'll bring out a few more memorable activities in those last two years of my 36 years at the Naval Academy. In the summer of 1990, we spent three weeks in Hawaii. The first week was on our own at a condo on island Kauai. I don't recall such beautiful scenery and variety elsewhere. The rainy side is lush with jungle greenery and beautiful flowers. At the edge are high cliffs with the pounding surf below. There was a place we could drive down to the beach and swim. The center of Kauai is a high mountain up into the clouds with the very highest rainfall anywhere, over 400 inches per year. We rented a helicopter ride to see the top—no roads! Well, the helicopter followed a ravine with spectacular waterfalls up as far as possible. Apparently the top is only open a few days each year. When we hit heavy clouds with rain, we had to turn back for a view of the coast.

Driving our rented car over to the opposite side of Kauai was like entering Arizona. It not only was desert with cacti, but also had a canyon of bright red rocks, similar to the Grand Canyon, only not as deep. You would have difficulty believing the change from most wet to all dry! The wind direction causing the weather pattern is most significant.

The next weeks we stayed on the island of Oahu, the main island, and participated in another Elderhostel. The Elderhostel organization has local experts, mostly from the university, speak on history, customs, botany and attractions. The tour guides drove our group, maybe 30, around the entire island in a bus for spectacular sightseeing. We saw the early king's palace, snorkeled over fish reefs, tried hula, and made leis. We even tasted poi, but didn't care for the taste. On our own, we took the island bus to an evening orchid show. We asked for 4th of July fireworks, but received a stare—4th of July is not at all of interest there.

Part of our trip was a flight over to the big island, named Hawaii. There we had another bus to circumnavigate the island and drive up to the top of the famous volcano, Kilauea. There are permanent observatories on top for astronomy. We walked up to the edge of the cauldron to see the rising smoke from the molten center far below. We also walked through places like caves where previous flows had gone and hollowed out the surface soil. A special stop was at a beach with "black sand." The sand is just broken lava. The bus driver raved over a drive through a plantation because the trees arched over the road. We thought—that's just like the entrance to Loch Haven, no big deal! But palm trees don't shade a road, so it was unusual for there. Another stop was an orchid farm.

In the winter of 1991, we got in our usual ski trips to slopes in Pennsylvania and out in Colorado. The summer was unusual in that we stayed at home for our local swimming and boating. Eileen and her son Kevin, only a year old stayed with us all summer. Her Jim was in Saint Petersburg, Florida, doing a clinical for his optometry degree. That was one of the few years we did not take a major trip to somewhere in the world.

As already noted, I retired from teaching at the Naval Academy in January 1992, after 36 years in the math department. We immediately took advantage of the new free time by taking two ski Elderhostel weeks. Elderhostel is a fun and educational program designed for seniors. It sponsors weeks all over the world for the local activities, plus lectures from their experts on a great variety of topics, including customs, history, geology, politics, and whatever is special in that region.

One of these weeks was at Auberge Escapade resort outside of Montreal, Canada. It was near the base of famous Mount Tremblant in Quebec. Part of our every day activities was skiing with instructors on the mountain. I particularly liked the long downhill runs of over a mile. The lectures were both interesting and informative. We learned a lot about Canada.

The other week was at Red Fox Ski Lodge near Smuggler's Notch in Vermont. Smuggler's Notch is actually on the back side of the more well-known ski area at Stowe, Vermont. These are gorgeous mountains with top notch skiing. We had beautiful weather, except very, very cold. Our ski instructor was surprised that our group showed up for class because he figured these old folks would stay back in the lodge. The lectures were informative. We learned the story of the "old man in the mountain," a natural rock outcropping that did look like a man's face.

Retirement was a blessing that meant Margaret and I could go anywhere we wanted, any time we wanted, and do anything we wanted (such as skiing and learning). For the next two or more generations, I might mention that having invested in the stock market over a 50 year period and accumulating an ample pile of money made it possible that any travel with expenses could easily be paid! That is the way to live and retire! When fall rolled around in 1992 and schools reopened, it occurred to me that this was the first year since I was 3 years old that I wasn't preparing for school!

That summer of 1992 was too busy to notice any change of pace. In fact it's been that way all along every year since, right up to this day.

The month of June was a major family reunion of the entire Wolfe Clan, all planned by sweet Margaret. We entertained over 40 descendants of the four children from John Calvin Wolfe Senior and Mary Elizabeth Redlin Wolfe, my grandparents. The central event was a cookout, along with every reasonable side dish, held at a special pavilion in Quiet Waters Park, in Annapolis on the north side of South River. Our current house is on the south side of the river across the water from Quiet Waters. The relatives came here from Florida, Ohio, Connecticut, Pennsylvania, Tennessee, Virginia, and of course, Maryland. Cousins by the dozens, some never here before, showed up to fellowship. This size get together won't happen again because now many of them have gone on to glory with our Lord.

In July, Margaret made her usual trip to Los Angeles to visit her sister, Elizabeth. Elizabeth was now living in a retirement hotel as their parents were with the Lord and the old homestead in San Marino had been sold.

August, that summer saw Margaret and me at another Elderhostel in Canada near Niagara Falls. We were on a spectacular cliff, escarpment, over the river and enjoyed the lectures: Flora and Fauna, geology, and philosophy. Of course, we took the ferry up to the falls in the mist.

The next month, September, was a trip to St. Petersburg, Florida on the Gulf Shore beach to celebrate Margaret's birthday, number 60. We visited well-known Busch Gardens and the Florida Thibodeau/Summers family. Also, we had dinner with my cousin, Bud Stark and his wife in St. Petersburg. Our condo was right on the beach of the Gulf of Mexico, where we swam every day and hiked up and down the sandy beach on the coast.

When finally at home, Margaret and I square dance, swim at the Naval Academy pool, take an aerobics class twice a week, and officiate at the local chapter of Full Gospel Businessmen's Fellowship. At church, I also impersonated a Methodist Circuit Rider, complete with costume and toy horse. I took up archery out in my yard, an activity which hadn't happened since childhood.

Wow! Do you think retirement is a bore? Just try to find time to read the daily newspaper!

Retirement was a great change in my life. Suddenly Margaret and I could do whatever we wanted the rest of the year. We had always traveled during summers, but were confined during the school year all those years of teaching. Now we could go places in the winter, the spring, or in the fall. We immediately took full advantage of the wealth of opportunities.

We took to extensive skiing the first winter of 1992. My son, Norman, had taught me to ski in the late 70's. He learned to ski with our church youth fellowship while a teen. Actually the youth went to Vermont and learned on the tough slopes with their youth mentor, an avid skier. Norman was smart to get Mom and Dad into it, because then we took the family out skiing on holidays. At the time, Cynthia was off at college, Western Maryland College, from 1976 to 1980. With Norman and Eileen, it was mostly the four of us skiing. Cynthia did pick it up after her graduation, as we went during Christmas vacation. Anyway,

Norman broke me in at Jack Frost, a small resort in PA, in the Pocono mountains. I was already 50 years old, so while I caught on fast, I never got really good at it. The children all got expert, especially Norman, who could ski anything including the bad moguls. They are all skiing today along with all grandchildren.

CHAPTER 13

Major Overseas Trips

I often tell my grandchildren a story of life. "Life is like a large book with a great many pages. If you stay in one place, you are living on one page of the book. To see the rest of the book, you need to travel all around the world." (Adapted from St. Augustine)

Well, our big retirement tour in 1993 was an Elderhostel sponsored trip to Kenya, Africa, our first time on that continent. We flew from New York to Rome, Italy, changed planes and flew on to Nairobi, Kenya. It was close to 24 hours to get to the hotel in Nairobi, exhausted. So tired, I left my cap in the taxi to the hotel. It was gone! We recovered from the plane ride quickly, and introduced ourselves to our Elderhostel group of 22, and began sightseeing. We toured the city in a bus and found an interesting example of local entrepreneurship. We passed crews of workmen filling potholes in the road, and beside them a sign that they were just volunteers, and needed donations. We heard that at night, the same crew dug out the paving stones so that they could do the same holes over again the next day!

The three weeks in August while we were there, we were treated like British royalty. The British had ruled Kenya until 30 years before we arrived. Kenya was celebrating 30 years of independence. So the locals spoke English with a heavy British accent. (Margaret: I claim that since they chased the British out, they had to learn English from textbooks, and therefore attempted to pronounce words the way they are spelled—a major disaster.) At one lecture, the speaker went on and on about "a-GRI-kul-tjur." Towards the end we figured out the topic was agriculture.

Our beds were made each day, and turned down at night, toilet paper specially folded, and dinners served in 5 separate courses with separate silverware for each course. I particularly liked the opening hot soup course, usually pure broth so it wasn't actually filling. And it was liquid that we needed since we could drink only bottled water otherwise. Dinner was the evening entertainment, ending after dessert and a final course of hot tea.

We traveled around the countryside to visit five game preserves: The Ark, Nakuru Park, Masai Mara Park, Ambroselli, and Tsavo. We observed game mostly from a Toyota van with an open sunroof. I took pictures of all the wild animals in their natural habitat. At the Ark, an observation building built like an ark and next to a salt lick, an alarm was set off any time in the night when an unusual animal came by so that we could jump up out of bed to go to a glassed viewing station. Among other sights, we saw a large rhino with her baby at the salt lick.

Our group toured each preserve in 3 separate vans (lorries) with open tops. I leaned out the top and took pictures of lions, just 5 feet from the camera on the edge of the road (actually a dirt path). I never would have believed we could get so close, just a few feet, from huge wild animals. I took hundreds of pictures, many close, of every native animal. I got one of a rare black panther. The guide said he hadn't seen one in many years. A family of white rhinos walked right in front of our van, several adults with a baby. "White" is an Anglicized word corrupted from the German "Weis", meaning wide—for its wide snout. The black rhino has a narrow snout.

We encountered (I have the pictures): herds of elephants, numbering 24 or more; zebras and wildebeests (gnus) in uncountable herds; the ugly warthog; baboons; monkeys of all sizes; hyenas (several gorging on a zebra), a den of hyena cubs; lions; cheetah; giraffes; Oryx; topi; impala; Grant's gazelle, as well as Thompson's Gazelle. The most fearsome and deadly animal was the Cape buffalo. It might charge and turn your car over. In the rivers were peaceful looking hippos and crocodiles, although they can be aggressive. In fact in Africa, more people are killed by hippos than by any other animal.

The most impressive sight to me was Mount Kilimanjaro. It is a massive white topped cone rising over 20,000 feet. What makes the mountain so spectacular is you see most of its height above the flat savanna. It's not just a peak in a high ridge of mountains. I understand Mt. Kilimanjaro is the largest free standing peak in the world. Of course the top is permanent snow, despite being close to the equator.

I have a picture of Margaret on another ridge outside of Nairobi with one hand on the sign saying "Equator," with a horizontal line going across the sign. She is wearing her heaviest clothes with a thick sweater. Did you think the equator was hot in August? Not at 5,000 feet up.

The accompanying lectures let us in on culture, volcanic origins, the independence fight, political unrest, and the economic dilemmas. The huge British plantations had been divided up, giving pieces first to the residents, who then divided it again as their sons grew up, so that it had come to the point that none could make a living by farming because the farms were too small. So much for equality! At the end of the Eldershostel, we went on to the coast at the Indian Ocean and visited Mombasa. We stayed at a villa on the water, so I swam in the Indian Ocean. Margaret and I each had a brief camel ride there on the sandy beach. We saw historic sights where Portuguese explorers had landed 'way back in the 15-hundreds. All thrilling new experiences before returning to Nairobi for the flight home.

That year, 1993, as in every year, we traveled around our country to visit the expanded family. We flew to Denver to visit Norman and his wife Nancy and their three kids for skiing and Christmas. We flew to Florida and enjoyed Eileen, who was pregnant with Karen, along with husband Jim and the two boys, Kevin and Jason. More frequently we saw the Behm family, Cynthia and Greg, along with their 3 boys right here in Maryland.

The years 1994 and 1995 were filled with local activities and our trips to Florida and Denver. Margaret made a trip each year to LA to visit her sister, Elizabeth. We went skiing both in PA with the Behms, and in Colorado with the Norman Wolfe family. Our ninth grandchild, Karen Summers, came on board in June 1994.

Another short trip was a drive to Knoxville, Tennessee to visit my cousin Bettie Anne Logan and her husband, Ed. The Logans have four married children, Joellyn, Eddie, Randy, and Melanie, whom we also enjoy on our visits, along with many grandchildren.

Thus we were busy with family visits both ways, them coming here as well as us going there. On trips here, I took all the families out fishing on the Chesapeake Bay. We all really enjoy the water and boating. We were allowed to keep our boat across the street at Dick Edward's house. Our senior exercise class sponsors interesting trips for shows and plays. For example we went to Pennsylvania for "Living Waters," a water jet show, and also the play "Noah."

The year 1996 was a big year with two major trips. In January, we got out of the cold while on a second trip to Hawaii. On this trip we added the island of Maui, as well as the previously visited islands: Oahu, Kauai, and Hawaii. The trip was taken with our area square dancers, so we danced with the local residents on each island as well as sightseeing. We had a great time! Back home we got in our usual skiing with the Behms and the Wolfes. New was introducing Greg Behm to skiing. He learned quite fast. In March, we flew to Florida during the children's spring break for the yearly visit to Eileen and family.

The second major trip was in April to the Holy Land with another Elderhostel group. All my life I've wanted to see the places talked about in the Bible, especially where Jesus walked and talked. This experience was my top priority in retirement and certainly didn't come up short.

We had two weeks in Israel, plus an added on week in Egypt on a different tour. It wasn't the best of times as the locals were essentially at war. Every day the Israeli jets flew over our heads on their way to the Lebanon border to bomb the Arabs. Our plane landed in Tel Aviv, from there we were bussed to Jerusalem and on to our Kibbutz on the eastern shore of the Sea of Galilee. A kibbutz is a cooperative where everyone works for the group and is then well taken care of for life. This Kibbutz, started back in the 1920's, sponsored tourism with a large number of individual cabins right on the shore of the lake. Margaret and I had our own cabin and could walk right down to the shore and go swimming. Yes, I swam in the Sea of Galilee!

The eastern shore of this sea is a narrow strip of land, often less than a mile wide, right under the Golan Heights. From the top of the cliffs, a 1000 feet or more up, you had a view and a dominant position over the farmlands below. The Arabs, from the formation of Israel in 1947 to the war of 1967, could and did lob shells down on the helpless people of the Kibbutz. The pockmarks in the walls are still there. The people had to work with guns at their sides, and the children were kept overnight in a communal dormitory with guards outside! The liberation war of 1967 took over the Golan Heights for Israel. That ended the shelling. If you were ever there, viewing the situation, you would agree that Israel should never give up control of the Golan Heights. It's unthinkable for those down below!

Our Kibbutz was called Ein Getti, where we stayed in our two-person personal cabin for one week. Every day our tour guide took us on a tour in a bus to all the sights around the Sea. We covered the entire shoreline, usually rough and rocky and recalled the Biblical events relating to each site.

One place on the eastern shore, where there was a gentle slope running down to the water, was clearly the place where Jesus sent the evil spirits into a herd of pigs that then charged into the water. The story HAD to refer to those people living at that very place. It was the only shore with a gentle slope to the water.

The entire Sea of Galilee is roughly 4 miles wide and 7 miles long, emptying into the Jordan River that is the border of Israel and Jordan. That river continues right down to the Dead Sea, which is well below sea level. The Sea of Gallilee has had various names, like the Tiberian Sea and now something else. Our guide told us not to stray on our own, even with a map, because the names, besides being in Hebrew, might not correspond to the names on our map.

One of the day trips was to the town of Capernaum where Jesus centered His ministry. He may have had a house, or been given a place in town. The fishermen Peter and Andrew had their home in Capernaum and their boat on the shore, just a stone's throw away. We saw the foundation stones of Peter's house, still in place. Today there is an open roof over the site to keep it from further weathering. Also in town is the shell of an old synagogue. That is probably the same location as the original synagogue in which Jesus healed the man with the withered arm. Remember Jesus saying, "On the Sabbath Day is it better to do good or to do evil?"

Just outside of Capernaum, we viewed the hill where Jesus taught and the teachings are now called The Sermon on the Mount. What a thrill, just to be there! Finally, we took a boat ride across the Sea, in a boat that was supposed to look and sail like Peter's boat. It was built in the same way except that it had a motor. Our ride was from the western shore across to our Kibbutz on the eastern shore At the dock were similar oats still used for fishing in the Sea. As a matter of fact, at the dock restaurant, I ate a "St. Peter" fish, a small bass caught in the lake.

One day-trip took us up to the Golan Heights to an old Roman bath. Part of it was ruin, but part was in use. Under Arab custom, the women had one part to themselves—Margaret wore her swimsuit and went in to that covered cave part. The men had several pools to use outside, which is where I got in. One site on the Heights was like a fort on a cliff. The story of this fort is that it was besieged for a long time until the defenses gave out. Before the enemy got in, all inhabitants jumped off the cliff so that there were none to capture. We just can't imagine living in those ancient times!

From Ein Getti, we bussed on south to Jericho, where Jesus gave sight to the blind man who called out from the side of the road. From Jericho it is all up hill to Jerusalem, about 50 miles away. The way is still mostly desolate and rocky land with only a few goat herders still living there.

Our final week was in Jerusalem, the Holy City. We stayed at the King David Hotel, just outside the wall of the old city, a very Jewish hotel. On the Sabbath, the elevators were automated to stop at every floor—so you wouldn't have to push a button. Breakfast in the dining room was all prepared the day before. Eggs were pre-boiled. There was no toast because the machine required a push button. There was no fresh bacon, and nothing fresh cooked. Our box lunches had been made the night before.

115

As all the local sites were closed for Sabbath, our tour took us out of town. Our guide nervously watched the orthodox Jews with their dark hats and long hair because they might decide to stone the bus for violating the Sabbath. However, we had no friction. We went to the Dead Sea to the cliff that was the foundation for the fortress called Masada. King Herod built the fortress as a retreat in case Roman politics turned against him. It was atop a long winding path to a high cliff. Water came from a system of troughs and cisterns. It was fairly impregnable. Herod died before he needed the retreat. In 70 AD Jews, chased out of Jerusalem, captured the fortress by stealth, and defied the Roman army. The Jews were families, old, young, children, adults, men and women. They managed to live there for about three years. The Romans decided that they couldn't allow these outlaws to continue, so they sent an army to destroy them. The army laid siege for a while and decided the fortress could hold out almost indefinitely. Herod had planned it well. So the army engineers began to build a slope to allow their battering machines to travel up to the walls. You can imagine the people looking out each day at the progress of the building, and counting the days until their defeat. So the evening before the battering rams could be hauled into place, ten men, who were the ranking officials, met to decide what to do. If the Romans took the place, the women would be made slaves, the men would probably be killed or paraded through the streets of Rome as examples of Roman power, the children would be enslaved or killed. They decided to not be taken. They set about killing all inhabitants, their own families included, they set fire to the stores of food, and they met together in one of the rooms. One man had to stab to death his 9 fellow men, and then commit suicide. So when the Romans broke through the next day, they found . . . nothing. It was an empty victory. That is the story of Masada. Fortunately we had a ski gondola to take us up the cliff to the top, although we could see some hardy souls climbing the steep trail.

Of course we toured the old city of Jerusalem inside the stone wall, walked the Via Della Rosa and the impressive temple mount. The top of the temple mount is now covered with an Islam Mosque. Inside the mosque, which one enters in stocking feet, guarded by an iron railing, is the huge more or less flat rock sacred to three religions. That rock is where Abraham almost sacrificed his son Isaac. It is the thrashing floor that David bought for a place to worship God. His son Solomon built the great temple there that lasted until the Babylonians under King Nebuchadnezzar burned and destroyed it in 586 BC. By the way, I heard that the stone temple was burned when the army stuffed soaked wood into all the cracks and seams of the great rocks. When the fire changed all that soaked water into steam, the steam expanded 1700 times in volume, causing violent explosions. These explosions, that could be heard as far away as Jericho, brought the temple walls down. Who says you need dynamite or modern explosives to blow something up!!!

Nehemiah led a group of returnees from Babylon to rebuild some of the old temple. The old timers simply cried over the weak results.

So the site is sacred to Jews. It is also sacred to Christians. The great builder, King Herod The Great, built a temple on the foundation rock of the Temple Mount that was one of the wonders of the world. Herod died in 4 BC, so this was just the generation before Jesus. Jesus walked there and taught on the temple steps. Jesus predicted that this great temple would be gone before the end of his generation. It happened, as He predicted, in 70AD under the siege of Jerusalem led by Roman general Titus. So goes the history of man, destroying the greatest monuments and architecture of all previous generations. I still cry!

As I said, the current building is sacred to a third religion. The Muslims say that Mohammed came to that rock and it was from there that he flew up to heaven. They say a depression in the rock is his footprint. So the rock is central in their building "The Dome of the Rock." The dome is massive and gilded and dominates the pictures of Jerusalem.

We stood before and I touched the great rock blocks that used to be the temple foundation. It is now called the "wailing wall." Many Jewish men go there to pray and to tuck into cracks little pieces of paper naming their prayer requests. Only men could approach the wall. Women had to stand back away. The blocks are enormous, maybe 30 feet long and 10 feet high, weighing untold tons. You figure out how the ancients put them in place. The story was that Herod, as the Roman appointee, had to ask permission of the Roman Senate to build the temple. He feared that they might not grant him permission if they thought the temple might somehow detract from the glories of Rome. So he sent a messenger with the request for permission, but he sent him by land, instead of the fast way by ship, and told him to take his time. Three years later the messenger returned, but the temple was already built. So what could Rome do if the senate didn't like Herod's plan!

At one time, about 1960's, Jerusalem was under Muslim control and Jews were not allowed into the city. But the Jews wanted to make the pilgrimage to Jerusalem. So a hotel on the outskirts of the city constructed a scale model of the old city with the buildings and walls in place. This scale model covers a full city block. Now archeologists use it to keep up with each new bit of information that they uncover. We walked around the model admiring the overview.

Outside of one of the closed gates into Jerusalem, archeologists have cleared an old stone staircase, perhaps one that Jesus used. Down hill, they are now clearing an area that used to be the city in King David's time. One archeologist thinks she has found King David's Palace.

One other site outside the old city showed a number of reconstructions of Biblical references. We saw an ox cart, crosses like those the Romans used to crucify—really just old olive trees. We saw an olive press, a sheep enclosure, a watch tower (built to house a guard to make sure no one stole those sheep) and we sat around a low table and learned how the last supper would have been. Actually, we were supposed to recline, but our host said Europeans absolutely couldn't eat in a reclining position. By reading the Bible carefully, plus using cultural clues, the host could tell us where Jesus and several of the disciples would have sat—and not where Leonardo Da Vinci thought. We did eat a simple meal at this table, but while sitting on a bench.

One day our bus took the group to Bethlehem, just several miles below Jerusalem. The main church is built right over the spot where they figure Jesus was born. Down in the basement, there is a small cave that is set to look like such a spot. At least it invigorates your imagination. The church itself is truly amazing. On the outside, on a ledge, going up to a lower window is a ladder, one of a construction type. They say that ladder has been untouched for well over a hundred years. There are competing factions or sects that manage the church. They will not touch the ladder because that would mean they are responsible for that wall of the church! Well, I suppose the ladder is still there! In a Bethlehem shop I bought several small olive wood carvings of a camel. One of them is an exceptionally fine piece of art and sculpture. It is on a shelf in my living room today.

This trip was a must for me and is recommended for everyone. I can only tell you what we saw. I can't convey the deep impressions on my mind and my heart!

Now, to move on, we flew out of Tel Aviv to Cairo, Egypt for an extended week. We relaxed in a downtown hotel. This time there were only a few of the previous group with us—the ones who had added on the Egypt trip. A local flight took us south near the southern tip of Egypt not far from the Aswan Dam. We saw the great stone carvings that had to be moved to higher ground because of the dam construction. They are thousands of years old and maybe 25 feet high. We were not allowed to take a picture of the dam. It was too secret?

Just below the dam, we started our riverboat trip down the great Nile River. We passed small sail boats and other small rowing crafts that could have been from any age. It was like stepping through history. One of the ancient temples we went through was on an island in the river. I have the pictures on color slides.

A main stop and really huge set of temples was at Karnack. The greatest building, meant to rival the pyramids, was by the exceptional pharaoh who declared only one God—Aton. He removed all the old Egyptian Gods in spite of their thousands of years in place. Well, so much for an innovator. This Pharaoh's very son took over and restored the old gods. Actually, the jobs of the huge number of priests depended on the many gods and donations by citizens to each one. It appears that the pressure of the priests aided the decision to reinstate the old religions. What will one do for a job?

The main obelisk at Karnack was over 100 feet tall, maybe 120. It had been carved on the surface, all the way to the top, with the exploits of the

Pharaohs. It was one solid piece of stone, granite, and was carved out of a stone mountain nearly a mile away. As far as I know, we do not have any piece of machinery today that can lift or move that obelisk. The Egyptians did it by hand! Do we have any engineers today as wise as the ancient Egyptian engineers? You can marvel at the exceptional accomplishments of science today. I marvel at what we accomplished back 3 to 5 thousand years ago!

Our cabin on the riverboat was below the main deck and engine diesel fumes from the rafted together boats seeped in. The fumes made Margaret sick and she missed the final big excursion. That trip was to the Valley of the Kings, on the east side of the Nile, right up to the nearby mountains. The Valley of the Kings was the burial site of a great many of the Egyptian rulers, along with some queens. A large temple with dozens of columns across the front was to honor one queen. There were innumerable steps up to the front entrance with carved lions along both sides.

We did go down into one of the tombs, all below ground, to the burial site. The walls along the way were painted with figures and scenes, the bright colors still visible. The tomb room was mostly empty. The treasures in general had been removed in prehistoric times by robbers, and what remained, when discovered, was taken to museums. I believe the temperature that day in Valley of the Kings was 105 degrees farenheit.

The big discovery, in the 1920's was King Tut's tomb. It hadn't been robbed and everything was there. The mummy, along with half a dozen of nested encasements was all at the Cairo Museum of History. The museum also displays Tut's pure gold mask and innumerable treasures buried at the site. Of course, we viewed all this and much more at the museum while in Cairo.

While back in Cairo, we took trips to various pyramids. The earliest, down near the Nile delta was in tiers. Each tier was smaller up to the top tier—flat on top. Elaborate passageways led underground to the burial chamber beneath. Queens were buried in separate pyramids, much smaller.

The great pyramids were on the desert at Giza, just outside of Cairo—three of them. The largest, in the center, is close to 300 feet high. It has a square base with 4 triangular faces, up to a pointed top. The faces were originally filled in with limestone to be glistening white and smooth. Five thousand years later, after all the pilfering of materials, they are now rough with base rocks exposed. From the bottom, the top still looks pointed. The enormous blocks on the lower levels weigh an unbelievable number of tons. They were quarried in the mountains, floated down the Nile on barges, and rolled to the site on logs. We are still guessing how levers lifted them into place. It is possible that each layer was covered with dirt (sand) and that after reaching the top, the millions of cubic yards of soil had to be removed. Imagine financing that job today!

We walked through the tunnel inside that great pyramid down to the throne rooms. No one was allowed into those inner rooms. It was a most impressive experience all along the way. We could see the hieroglyphs and paintings on the walls.

Another event was the camel ride outside on the desert. The camel squats on the sand while you climb up into a saddle. Margaret and I both rode camels. You hang on for dear life as the camel gets up, hind legs first, pitching you forward. Then the front legs come up, leveling you off. It was a bumpy ride, more so than on an elephant. I enjoyed the novelty. We also walked around the equally well-known Sphinx. It has a man's head and a lion's body, apparently carved out of existing rock. The very size is surprising, as it's like walking around a city block. You must see my pictures of these world wonders.

We flew from Cairo back to Tel Aviv, and then on to Kennedy airport in New York. El Al airline gave all of our group a hard time leaving, and we sat in the airport for a long delay, apparently because some high official was flying out at the same time. This trip is an absolute must for anyone who wants to experience the wonders of the world first hand.

Of course, the overseas trip was not the entire year. The rest of the year was filled with many small trips to keep up with our family and friends. In May of this year, 1996, we flew to Denver for the Masters graduation of Norman from University of Denver. We took Cynthia with us to the 50th wedding anniversary of Ed and Bettie Anne Logan in Knoxville, TN. Most of the summer I was growing vegetables in the garden and swimming in our South River.

In the fall, we hiked the Shenandoah valley and surrounding mountains in Virginia for 3 days. Finally in November, we sailed on a Celebrity cruise in the Caribbean, sponsored by our senior exercise group. We visited new places like Caracas, Venezuela, Aruba, Guadeloupe, Puerto Rico, St. Thomas and Granada. Activities included snorkeling over the reefs with clouds of brilliant fish. In each port, we toured the island with all its local sights, magnificent scenery and flowers. Our ship was named Zenith.

No small feat every year for 50 years was canning about 50 quarts of prize peaches off our single peach tree! The canning was always at the end of August—the hottest part of the summer!

One major trip in 1997 was hiking in the Canadian Rockies, which are an extension of the U.S. Rockies, up the western coast of Canada. Under the care of Tauck Tours, we flew into Calgary, a good sized modern city. We were impressed with how the buildings in the shopping district were connected with covered bridges—to avoid deep snow drifts. The bus ride from there took us up to Banff National Park and by Lake Louise. Louise is one of the prettiest lakes anywhere.

Overnight we stayed at Emerald Lake Lodge, right on another gorgeous lake. It is a cloudy green because of the chemicals washed down from the glacier that feeds it. The next day our bus went up to a plateau used for landing helicopters. After boarding us, our helicopter flew to the Bobbie Burns Lodge up near the top of one of those rugged all rock mountains. The lodge is accessible only by helicopter. All supplies have to be flown in. In particular, there is no telephone or mail. You are very close to nature and certainly in the height of wilderness.

Actually the lodge had excellent accommodations with a big dining room and great views. They issued our hiking gear, expecting us only to bring normal clothes. We got an insulated, hooded jacket, wind pants, heavy hiking boots, a rain poncho, and a backpack along with a water bottle. We kept all this gear until the day of departure. They didn't issue personal bug repellent, but had some out each day and we really needed it! The mosquitoes were impossible to deter.

Our group stayed at Bobbie Burns for 3 days and nights. Each day was a new experience in itself. You started each day by boarding a small helicopter, maybe five riders along with the pilot. It was a challenge to get on board in the windstorm from the rotor, an all new exciting experience. The helicopter took us up to a ridge or a small spot near the top of a mountain—a different spot each day. The landing spot might not be much bigger than the helicopter!

The good news was that our day's hike was always across a ridge or down hill. Just imagine the first pioneers who had to climb up!

We carried our lunch and water in our backpack. Lunch was usually eaten on a rock or meadow along the way. Sometimes the helicopter came back and took us to a different mountain for the afternoon hike, probably several miles away. The higher terrain was barren rock and had snow, while some levels had soil and wild flowers. Remember we hiked downhill, a real convenience.

One day we hiked across a glacier several hundred feet thick. You had to use extreme care to stay back from the cracks in the ice. Some were very wide maybe a foot or so. In fact, July was the earliest the hiking guide dared take us on a walk on the glacier because the snow had to be melted enough to see the cracks. A snow bridge might cave in over an unseen crevasse. Our hiking guide knew the safe routes. I looked down one crack maybe 100 feet deep with perhaps water at the bottom. If you fell in, you would never get out! A rescuer couldn't pull you out before you froze.

Our full group at the lodge was 40 people, mostly middle-aged couples. We were divided up into a half dozen groups of 6 or 7 with a guide, the most that would fit in the helicopter. On an incline as we hiked, my guide said that I went up like a jackrabbit. It was all walking, no tooth and nail stuff. Of course, we stopped frequently just to look: the snowy peaks, huge rocks, deep valleys, green moss, colorful wild flowers, and expansive wilderness. Note that we were in the center of that mountain range, not the eastern or western slopes. Very few people have ever seen that territory, but I sure do recommend it.

Next, we took a big helicopter to the Bugaboos Lodge for the following three days and nights. The Bugaboos was just like the Bobbie Burns Lodge, with the same facilities. Our helicopter flights each day were very similar to the previous ones except that we were in a new set of mountains with all new views. There was some evidence of wildlife, small animals and birds. I only remember the soaring birds. I talked to one of the main guides who came there from Switzerland. He was right at home and did the difficult fingernail climbing. He had another small, younger group, which did do the rock climbing with ropes. Our guide was one of the local women who took the intermediate group.

I should mention that this enterprise is year round. In the winter the helicopters take skiers to the very tops of slopes, from which they must ski all the way down to the valley below. I saw some of the skis they use. Those skis are about a foot wide!

Good things always seem to come to an end, but then there are more and better things ahead. On the eighth day, we were bussed back to a hotel in Calgary, before the flight home. This whole trip was a Tauck Tours arrangement. The company is stationed in Westport Connecticut. I don't think you could do better.

Another big excursion happened in October 1997. We took a tour to China which lasted over two weeks. That was our first trip to the Orient, and an entirely different culture from our own. The trip was arranged by Vantage Deluxe World Travel, and we were with a group of some two dozen. We started from JFK in New York, flew to Vancouver, and from there on Cathy Airline to Hong Kong, arriving some 19 hours later. Since we crossed the International Date Line, we repeated one day. Naturally on the return flight we lost a day. It's not easy to keep your system in tune. (Margaret remarks: Carvel wasted a lot of time trying to figure out what the date was.)

In Hong Kong we immediately boarded a local plane to the Capitol, Beijing, for another 3 hours' flight. The first day at our hotel was "pull yourself together." Margaret's luggage lock had broken off, and we had been advised to lock the luggage, so she left the hotel to try to find a replacement. She spied a street lined with small outdoor kiosks. Of course no one spoke English. One of the vendors proudly pointed to her daughter who spoke English. However, "Lock" is not one of the normal vocabulary words. Margaret got across "small." The girl happily brought out baby clothes! Margaret did find a lock later on in another city.

The next day, early, we started touring with a bus to the Cloisonné Ware factory. They make exquisite vases of copper body with wire inlaid enamel, usually blue, and extensively intricate design. The process dates back to the Ming Dynasty, from years 1435 to 1504. Next on the tour were the Ming tombs, where we walked the "Sacred Way." I have pictures of the statues—full sized lions and elephants.

Our bus trip continued on to the Great Wall of China. It is one of the few man—made structures which can be recognized by our astronauts in space! The wall is wide enough (15 feet) to carry a chariot drawn by several horses. It is 24 feet high. Parapets line the tops of the walls and every few hundred yards is a defensive tower. The construction is phenomenal! And to think its length is over 3000 miles! The wall was started in the 7th century, but not finished in its present form until the Ming Dynasty. By the time it was completed it was obsolete because cannon had been invented. A cannon ball would pierce the wall part way and eventually breach the system. Most of the wall is in disrepair, but a part is restored for the tourists to see and walk on.

The next day we visited the Forbidden City, which is the walled emperor's palace of buildings. There are said to be 9000 rooms in the compound. If you visited just one room per day, it would take you 27 years to get through the palaces. Most of the buildings are yellow, or earth color. Only the emperor's personal building had a red tile roof and red walls, symbolizing celebration. The whole complex was built by one million laborers over a period of 40 years. It was used until 1924, although China became a republic in 1912. Besides the emperor, only women (the harem) and eunuchs stayed in the palace overnight. All distinguished visitors had to leave.

The emperor allowed the public into the outer court, but only exalted guests into the inner court. The emperor's large receiving hall had just one seat, the throne. Everyone else knelt on the floor, while incense burners flavored the air. The art and architecture are world-renown, although the treasures were looted by the Japanese in the 1930's and the Communist revolutionaries in 1949. The loyal Chinese retreated to Taiwan and still occupy that island.

Despite the elegance of the palace, Margaret checked out the ladies' room and was surprised. It contained a series of nicely partitioned and tiled holes in the ground. Carvel said the men's room was a wall to pee against, so the urine ran down to a trough.

I was impressed with Tiananmen Square, which is the largest public square in the world, over 100 acres. A million people can gather in the square. In the center of the square is a 118-foot obelisk whose cornerstone was laid by Mao, and then the obelisk completed in 1958. Around the square are: Mao's Memorial Hall, containing the preserved body of Mao for public view (we didn't view), The Great Hall of the People with an assembly room for 10,000 people and a dining room for 5,000 dinner guests, the Museum of China History, and also the Museum of the Chinese Revolution. We walked around the square and through the "Gate of Heavenly Peace" that was built in 1417. We were there shortly after the student's revolt and massacre in the square, and we were told not to mention it or express sympathy. The guards were all around, though they wouldn't let us take their picture, and they had recently deported a tourist for saying something about the massacre.

Besides European and American tour groups roaming about, Chinese tourists from the rural inland were snapping photos. They considered Caucasians to be curious, and one group asked to take a picture with Margaret. Our guide said that Chinese tourists were particularly intrigued by blondes.

I should mention that we ate like dignitaries at the hotel or top restaurants. In the restaurant, the food was on huge turntables in the center of round tables that seated some 20 people. The food was in large sculpted trays shaped like boats. The turntable rotated slowly by you so that it was possible to use your spoon to take a snack from each tray and put it on your individual plate. I think the spoons were a concession to westerners. The natives would use chopsticks and we were encouraged to try to use chopsticks. I could seldom recognize what I was eating. One dish was called "Peking Duck." It was billed as a really special dish. Everyone got a chunk of very oily carved duck, skin and all. I am allergic to poultry fat, and began to peel off the skin, much to the outrage and horror of the waiter, who insisted that was the best part! At least we knew what that dish was. Other food was in nice chunks of unidentifiable origin with unidentified greens around them. The fish had bones—you could recognize that food.

Around town were thousands of bicycles. They had their own several lanes on the main roads. The bikes had huge luggage racks packed up high with merchandise, or groceries, or sometimes two or three people. They took the place of cars that were relatively few. Our guide, who spoke English very well, told us that success for the individual Chinese citizen was 5 C's: a Career, a Condo, a Credit Card, a Cell phone, and a CAR! Notice "Children" was not included!

We noticed two dramatic differences in China from our way of life. The first was the sky—always gray and never blue. We were told the haze was the result of smoke and pollution from so much burning of soft coal for cooking and heating, and the burning of fields to clear them of stubble. The other was the total lack of birds. The guide told us that all birds had been eaten. We later found that the government was part of the problem. When farmers complained about the birds eating their rice, the government offered a bounty for each pair of bird's feet turned in. Naturally all the wild birds were destroyed for food and money! Also, there were essentially no dogs or cats. (You can't keep a dog in an apartment 7 stories up. And the food is too expensive.) All pets were exotic birds kept in fancy cages. The local markets had a big business in selling these cages and also the mostly imported birds. Also, there were few trees, the ones we saw were small, newly planted, and practically no grass grew in the urban areas. All the large old trees had been cut down in the past for fuel and building material.

We flew from Beijing, 18 million people to Xi'an, 23 million people, in central China. Xi'an was the ancient capitol, going back 8,000 years to Neolithic times. It was the center of 11 dynasties, in particular the site of Emperor Qin Shi Huangdi (3rd Century B.C.) He was the one who placed a whole army of terra-cotta warriors underground near his tomb. They were discovered in 1974 and then uncovered so you can walk around and see in some of the tunnels the full sized men, horses, and chariots. Each warrior had its own face and head characterized so that it appeared to be a copy of an individual. Imagine doing as many as 6000 of these men, all painted and carefully crafted. Unfortunately many of these terra-cotta figures had been beheaded or toppled by subsequent raiders. The government is still in the process of restoring these pieces of art.

Carvel with terra cotta warrior in China 1997

We visited the Provincial Museum with its very old stone tablets etched with texts, and its collection of the terra-cotta warriors, and bronze carriages with terra-cotta horses. Also, on our tour was the "Flying Duck" pagoda, the tallest and best preserved pagoda. The guide told us that he had climbed to the top, all 228 steps. We just looked! The wood carving on the outside is just spectacular and intricate. Unusual is the wood construction. Nowadays in China, all building is block and cement. Because of the 5000 years of cutting, the wood, that is trees, is all gone.

Many of the buildings had carved or cast large lions in front. They are so stylized, you wouldn't recognize the animal. The guide said the artist had never seen a lion. He was working from a picture, which had been brought from a Buddhist pagoda in India. At the local zoo, we saw their three panda bears, a symbol of China today. Also, China is famous for jade carving, and I have a picture of several jade pieces standing up over my head. You wouldn't believe the workmanship.

One evening we attended a dinner theatre, seeing a multitude of Chinese dancers in gorgeous costumes perform their traditional dances. It was a great show, along with the very best food.

A highlight of our trip was a week-long river cruise on the Yangtze River, where we went maybe 1000 miles inland, as far as the river is navigable. The boat had nice cabins, good dining, and its own follies show in the evening. The Yangtze is the third largest river in the world at 3,910 miles. Only the Amazon and the Nile are longer. We started our voyage at Wu Han and went to Chong Quing, which is as far as large boats can go. With 258 passengers, our river cruiser was fairly large.

After a morning excursion to a museum, we steamed by the famous Three Gorges Dam. This huge dam contains the largest hydro-electric system in the world. It was still under construction and not operating. Our boat traveled through a canal made around the side of the big dam. The canal had a lock to raise the boat to a higher level. Northwest of the dam, we passed through each of the gorges. The river narrows and the sheer rock cliffs tower overhead in each gorge. We were probably the last year of visitors to see the depth of these spectacular gorges. When the dam closes, it will raise the water level 325 feet, submerging all the historic towns and sites along the way for 100 miles above the dam. I believe a million people have already been evacuated and some of the historic sites evacuated. When you go, you won't see what we saw! However, the dam is supposed to provide electricity so that people can have power more than occasionally, and also it is supposed to control the floods, which regularly kill millions of peasants.

At one place, we got off the river boat into small 10-person shallow draft sampans (like canoes), to go up a small stream for new thrills in the narrows. Part way, 4 barefoot, heavy legged laborers hauled the boats with ropes over rocky sand bars. That enterprise will also disappear when the dam raises the river level.

On one of the port stops along the river, we had dinner ashore and went to a show of acrobats, tumblers, jugglers, and a contortionist—all put on by a school dedicated to teaching these skills. The youths could bend over backwards, put their head between their legs, and look forward! They did balancing acts with several persons on top of one another, and all kinds of flips. I've never seen anything that extreme before or since! You would think that they didn't have bones, just soft connections!

Another stop was the ancient town of Jingzhou, a capitol for many Chinese kings for over 400 years. The most unusual sight was "Mr. Shue," an official who died about 2000 years ago and was embalmed, placed in several air-tight caskets, which were then placed inside of a large log, the size of a redwood. Today he is on view in a glass formaldehyde vat. He looks as if he died last week! Also gone are those huge trees.

At Chong Qing, we disembarked the river cruiser, climbing 200 steps up to the city. That city was the largest, some 32 million people. (It seemed like every city we came to was larger than the last, and none of them had we ever heard of!) It was raining, and the high altitude airport fogged in. So our airport bus drove to a new modern airport in the country, down a super highway. You would be very surprised at the latest rest stops. The man's side had a wall with a trough at the bottom. The women's side was just a hole in the tiled floor. There were no doors, and the stalls were just waist high. See our picture! The country-side looked lush, just like the tourist pictures of China, with very green rice paddies on terraces. The airport was billed as a "Civil Airport." Some things get lost in translation! Because our group luggage had increased in weight (terra cotta warrior souvenirs) our guide had to bribe the officials to get us on the plane.

The airplane flew us back to Hong Kong for a few days in the port city. The original port was an island off the coast. It was acquired by the British in the "Opium Wars" in 1842. The British also got Kowloon on the mainland. Later, more territory was annexed up to the present large area, which holds 6 million people. It was a haven during WW II for the Chinese fleeing the Communist take over. On June 30, 1997, the British returned the administration of Hong Kong back to the Chinese. At the time we were there, the locals claimed that they were operating under the same capitalist rules as before the turn over a year before. We wonder if it stayed that way.

We two regularly took the ferry across the harbor from our hotel in Kowloon to the island for sightseeing and shopping. We admired the forest of skyscrapers with names of familiar multinational companies. McDonalds had a kiosk in the local small city park! One day our tour had a bus ride up to the top of the high central mountains. Near the top, called Victoria's Peak, (you know who named that!) overlooking the harbor, were many mansions owned by the billionaires of Hong Kong. The world trade there creates the 8th largest economy in the world. Money flows like water! The view of the entire harbor was quite spectacular.

Another day, we took a harbor ride in a sampan to see the shipping and the "boat people." Thousands of poor people were living on the water, mostly in sampans. Their whole life is afloat. One afternoon we had "tea" at a top hotel, spending several hours gawking with our fellow tourists at the other customers. Along with the tea was a tower, holding a half dozen stacked round trays of exotic tidbits. They were tasty, but we had no idea what we ate! However, the bill was also spectacular! $40, as I recall.

We two also took the Star ferry at night to see all the lights. It was easy because the ferry was free for seniors.

Another time, we saw a bird street where the vendors sell the pet birds in lavish cages along with the bird food. That street was torn up, being repaved, and the old buildings around it are to be replaced with high-rise buildings—12 or so stories. Today you won't see bird street, at least not downtown. The old places are constantly giving way to the new.

I did make one major purchase in Hong Kong. On a tour of a jewelry store, I saw a gold ring with a beautiful red stone. The large stone was actually red coral from a reef off of Formosa Island. The ring fit and was an appropriate reminder of Hong Kong. The red coral is considered a precious gem, and also a disappearing resource. The ring has 8 small diamonds along the side. I bought it for something close to $2,000, and I wear it on various special occasions. This was the first time something cost me when going through U.S. customs back home. All other times, our purchases have been less than the $400 limit per person.

The plane out of Hong Kong went all the way to New York, an awfully long ride. But we gained back the day we had lost going over the International Date Line.

Our next big trip was in 1998 to Ireland, Scotland, and Wales with another Elderhostel group. The big advantage of Elderhostel is that you have daily lectures on the spot at each attraction. These lectures cover the history, culture, customs, and importance of each place. The lectures are given by experts, usually local professors of the local colleges. It is an eye opening education.

In Ireland, we stayed at an old estate in the refurbished castle (manor house), visiting the towns and ancient sites. Out on some fields were circles in the land, which could only be seen from overhead in planes. These areas were burial sites of ancient people back before the Romans came. Some excavation had revealed tombs and artifacts that could date the inhabitants. We stooped over and went into one of the tombs Of course it was empty. Also, in Ireland, we saw three local young girls perform the Irish step dancing, the most intricate foot work. The girls wore elaborate embroidered costumes, which are so expensive they are passed around in the dance clubs.

We took ferries across to Wales with our bus to continue to Scotland. By the way, the population of Wales had many more sheep than humans. The same bus and bus driver took our group through Ireland, Wales and Scotland, dodging sheep in very narrow roads.

In each country we were entertained by the music and dancing of local groups. Ireland, of course, had Irish dancing by young girls, and Scotland had their dancing in period costumes. Sometimes we went to theaters, and other times the groups came to us at our digs.

In Scotland, we stayed in Edinburgh and saw the King's castles, and also the place where the Queen of England stays when visiting. Nearby, we looked at the field where "Braveheart" led the successful charge against the English. A staggering amount of history was learned, and now mostly forgotten! I feel like I could take all these trips over again just to refresh my memory. Our tour bus continued north in Scotland through the moors and countryside. In particular, we saw the famous golf course at St. Andrew's where golf originated, and where the American and world golf champions play. The greenery, hills, lakes and rivers are all spectacular to see. We saw Loch Ness where the ancient sea monster is supposed to live. It was quiet and no monster. That was another trip of learning, history, art music, culture, geography, people and customs.

In the winter of 1998, we took our many ski trips, this time with each of the three families: Summers, Wolfes, and Behms. In spring we also took the Summers family to Longboat Key in Florida for a very enjoyable beach. Finally all four of our families got together at a beach home on the outer banks of North Carolina for a week of swimming. All nine of the grandchildren had a ball together. Actually, all summer, while at home here in Loch Haven I swam almost every day in the South River, usually by myself. South River is just an inlet from the Chesapeake Bay.

I had my first cataract operation and found it to be a huge success, greatly improving my vision. Margaret got an eye done in January of 1999. Eventually we both had the other eye done, also a great success.

By hooking up to internet and using e-mail, we got long descriptive messages from Norman at McMurdo sound on Antarctica, along with visits to the South Pole. Norman actually skied around the pole marking the South Pole. The ice shifts, so naturally the pole marker has to be moved each year. Norman worked there each fall, there spring, for several years, checking out the medical equipment and supplies, about a six-week stay. The doctors taking care of these Antarctica stations were hired by Norman. In particular, he hired Dr. Jerri Nielsen, the one who made news when she developed cancer and had to be flown out of the South Pole Early. She wrote a book on her experience and in it mentioned Norman. Normally no machinery can go in or out during the -50 to -100 degree winter temperature. An airplane would have its engine oil freeze.

I finished 15 years as president of the Annapolis chapter of the Full Gospel Businessmen's Fellowship. It was a blessing and an outreach for the men involved. Even though we no longer hold chapter dinners, I continue, in 2012, to have a breakfast or a picnic cookout here at my home each year for the remaining men.

We are up to 1999, a significant year with my back operation and our overseas trip to Alaska. We also went on our usual three ski trips with the three families. Margaret had a bad fracture in her left leg that January that she still blames on the skiing. What really happened is that for some unknown reason, she passed out in the shower room at home. Falling to the floor jammed the leg against the wall splintering that left leg. (Margaret says: That's Carvel's version. My version is that the week before, skiing on icy slope, I ran into a fence, cracking my goggles and smashing my leg. But I seemed ok then. Later, the night before the break, we were square dancing and I could feel that I was unsteady on the twirls and turns. Sunday morning, in the shower, I felt faint, but thought I should rinse the suds off before leaving the shower, but then my leg gave way. Carvel was in the kitchen working on breakfast and didn't hear my pleas for help. A woman who was staying with us, a sort of boarder, heard me and came to help. Between them they got me to a bed. I couldn't lift my left leg at all to get it on the bed. Carvel kept insisting that it must just be a bruise and would go away so I could attend church. I insisted on phoning 911. The boarder found a robe to throw over my naked body before I was transported to the hospital. At the hospital, the nurses were pleased that they didn't have to clean or undress me. That night, the doctor inserted a titanium rod in my leg from my knee to my ankle.

It's still there—2012) For the rest of the winter and most of the spring, she was on crutches. The bottom line is that Margaret gave up skiing for good. (Margaret adds: The doctor told me that if I had an accident with that leg that caused the rod to bend, I would be in major trouble— probably meaning a leg amputation. Anyhow, it was the third after ski season that I had been on crutches. It was time to quit!) Since then, I, Carvel, have been on my own skiing with the children.

Over the summer, we had visits at home from all three of the children's families. Those visits included both swimming and fishing, along with crabs from my crab pot. My cousin Kay Barrans and her husband, Dick, were here for their regular visits. This time, we took in the fourth of July fireworks in the harbor off the Naval Academy grounds.

By August, Margaret could get around ok and we were off to Alaska. That is another must see trip because the scenery is so striking. We took a Holland America cruise ship out of Vancouver, Canada, sailing up the coast to Skagway, Alaska. It was three pleasant days on board to Skagway, the site of the start of the Alaska gold rush in 1897. Around the small town, we visited the local hangouts, the theaters, the museums with artifacts and photos, all from those gold miners. Right in town, we boarded the small gauge railroad that took us on the tortuous climb over the surrounding mountains through White Pass Summit. The miners in 1897 had had to haul their heavy gear up that mountain pass on their backs, and many didn't make it. A few managed to buy horses to haul gear, but the land had no feed for the horses so they didn't last long. One ravine was named "Dead Horse Gulch" in memory of the starving horses that toppled over there to their death.

Up on the plateau where roads were possible, we switched from the train to a bus. The bus went from Fraser, Alaska into the Yukon Territory of Canada. Our guide said that the miners had to bring a designated amount of supplies up the pass. The Canadian Mounties made the rule because they didn't want all those gold prospectors dying in Canada over the winter. No one knew for sure where the boundary was between Alaska and Canada there.

We stopped at a game preserve called Yukon Wildlife to see fenced-in native wild animals: caribou, musk ox, Dahl sheep, mountain goat, moose, and other small animals. By the way, the bus, the preserve, the night's inns and restaurants were all owned by Holland America. What a monopoly!

Along the way was a stop at the Yukon capitol of Whitehorse and finally we drove into Dawson City. Dawson City, near the gold fields and near Yukon River, was the destination of the gold rushers. Those miners in 1898 spent the winter at Lake Bennett, where they built make-shift rafts or boats to cross the lake next summer to the Yukon River and on down river to Dawson. Dawson sits on permafrost, and so the ground stays frozen.

We boarded a riverboat, that is, our Holland America group of about 25 or 30, at Dawson to sail on down the Yukon River into Alaska. From the boat we caught another bus into Chicken, Alaska, a town with a permanent population of about 6. The early residents at Chicken wanted to name the town after the state bird, but they settled for Chicken because they couldn't spell Ptarmigan. I believe Chicken consisted of one restaurant aka rest stop (with tourist souvenirs), and about a half dozen houses. From there our bus went through Eagle and Tok to our destination, Fairbanks, a good sized City.

At Fairbanks, Margaret and I had signed up for a small plane ride scheduled to fly above the Arctic Circle to Nome to see total darkness, and to see some local Indians. Well, the fog was heavy and therefore our plane was canceled. The final lap in Alaska was on a regular railroad with observation cars to the port of Anchorage. On the way we stopped at Denali National Park for a day. The park bus took us deep into the wilderness where the driver pointed out the sights and animals. He told us that you rarely see all 4 of the big wild animals. We saw all 4: the moose, the caribou, the Dahl sheep with huge curved horns, and the grizzly bear. These animals were all wild and off the road, but close enough for a picture. It was an exciting experience!

Instead of another ship, we flew out of Anchorage on the way back home. Perhaps a couple more tidbits: Near Juneau, Alaska, we took a small boat to get up close to the famous Mendenhall Glacier. I saw calving of huge hunks of ice down the sheer cliff of ice into the bay. At one of the gold fields Margaret and I panned for gold using the soil that was given us. We actually got a few little flakes, worth about $12 at the time.

Fall 1999 was the time of a major back operation for me. It was my first such experience other than minor things like the cataract removal. Dr. Bands, the local back expert, did an outstanding job. He went into the lower back, relieving pressure by cleaning out the spinal column and removing bone spurs. A squished disc was reset and whatever needed to be done to help the back function ok was accomplished. I was in the hospital a few days afterwards and many more days at home in recovery. Today, 12 years later, I'm still skiing, dancing, exercising and keeping up! The back is not perfect, like in youth, but it holds up through all these activities. God has blessed me beyond any reasonable expectation!

CHAPTER 14

Years 2000 to 2004
Never a Dull Moment

Time flies along, but the speed comes from our extraordinarily full line of activities. We usher in the New Year on the dance floor with our square and round dance friends from many clubs. The dances are all called, or cued, by some of the best talent in the area. That means that the "caller" names each step or maneuver in unison with the music. Everybody on the floor does the same step at the same time, making a beautiful pattern. The New Year's dance runs from 9 PM till close to 1 AM.

Our winter trip in February of 2000 was to the island of Bequia in the south Caribbean, not far from South America. The best description of Bequia is "you can't get there from here." I'll stand by that! Our flight from Florida changed planes in Antigua. The local flight from Antigua to St. Johns was on an airline called LIAT, which the locals translated as "Leaves Island Any Time." In fact, we passengers were at the airport departure gate on the stated time, and sat for an hour waiting for the pilot and airline stewards to arrive—late. Then, the plane broke down and made an unscheduled landing, requiring passengers to wait in a small airport with absolutely NO information about when or if our flight would continue. So, our early afternoon flight to St. Johns turned into an evening flight. Now, the only way from St. Johns to Bequia was by the local ferry. The last ferry of the day was gone! A representative of our condo had been patiently meeting every flight all afternoon long. He drove us to a small island hotel, which fortunately had a room to rent us. We were scheduled to arrive at our resort on Saturday afternoon. Well, on Sunday morning our cab took us to the ferry, so our arrival was Sunday noon. On the dock, we kept looking for transportation to "The Plantation Resort." No one was there to meet us and take us to The Plantation. Finally the problem was cleared up—the name had changed to "The Palms Resort." We had a lovely private cabin near the water, and a private condo beach. We could hike the island and walk to a small commercial area. The dining room for the resort was in a palm-covered pavilion with a band playing. We walked the statue-lined paths to and from the main building. It was delightful, but a once in a lifetime experience that we do not plan to repeat. I've never been that lost or disconnected!

After our winter skiing, we took a driving trip to Tennessee in late spring. We picked up my cousins, Bette Anne and Ed Logan, plus their daughter Melanie Wilkerson and her daughter Jamie, and drove them all to Dallas, Texas. In Dallas, Eddie Logan was hosting the marriage of his son, Aaron, to Karen. It was a big family affair and a lovely wedding. We persuaded Bette Anne, in the interest of space conservation, to keep her luggage down to one bag and one hat for church. Margaret told her only the bride might wear gloves, and talked her out of taking several white pairs. She had to take a box of various pills and breakfast "foods" as she didn't eat what anyone else would for breakfast. Ed was in the early states of Alzheimer's, so the women were glad that I was there to shepherd him in and out of the men's room.

Over the summer, I flew to Florida for the Full Gospel Businessmen's annual convention. I have been a member of the local chapter for many years. And then, in October, I flew to Brownsville, Texas, to participate in one of their "fire teams." A fire team is a group of evangelists who wish to fire up the local people to accept Christ as Lord and go to the local churches for worship. My particular assignment was to the students at the University of Texas, at Brownsville. Others went around town to businesses, poor neighborhoods, and community groups. One Spanish speaking team went across the border to minister in Mexico. A main event was the giveaway of many hundreds of bags of groceries to the needy. The groceries were trucked in by a large truck and we passed the bags out in the center of town to poor families. That evening was an all-city convention with top-notch speakers.

In the University cafeteria, every day, I spoke to students, mostly one on one. Several of them agreed to go to a church and worship. One said he was transferring to Boston and would find a church in that town. Who knows what results come out of a Fire Team mission? Only God.

We entertained all of our children and their families at home in Loch Haven. At one time all 9 of our grandchildren were here together— quite a treat. Christmas day we spent with the Behms, near Westminster, Maryland, opening a huge pile of gifts.

Whatever the season, we are there for the cultural activities: the live plays at three local theatres, the opera, the five community concerts staged at Southern High, the Navy Band outdoor concerts over the summer, etc. Something is going on every week! You don't have to grow moss when you are old!

In October and November of 2001, we went on a delightful cruise down the west coast of Central and South America on the Holland America ship Ryndam. The start was a flight out of BWI airport to San Diego with a change of planes in Detroit. We were met by out tour leader and taken by bus to the port for boarding on ship. We had a very nice room with veranda on the Veranda Deck. I took many pictures on the ship and on all our shore stops along the way. By participating in ship activities, such as aerobics, stretch class, dance class, and early morning walking the promenade deck, we each earned enough points to collect a Ryndam T-shirt.

The first five days out of San Diego, we were at sea in the Pacific Ocean. A very dramatic event was our October 31 rescue of a jet skier who was out 25 miles from shore and 45 miles from the nearest port. He turned out to be a 17-year-old boy who had rented a jet ski from the beach at Acapulco. He ran out of gas and drifted for two days. It was near dusk on Halloween when a bridge officer scanning the horizon for whales saw him. If the officer hadn't seen him, that kid would not have made it back alive. He was no doubt dehydrated, exhausted and sun-burned. The big ship turned around, (with all the passengers watching from the various decks), went back, kept the Jet Ski in a spotlight in the dark, and launched a lifeboat to pick him and the Jet Ski up. The youth was turned over to the Mexican consulate at our next port, Puntarenas, Costa Rica. The consulate arranged for him to return home. Our Captain's comment was, "No doubt his mother will have something to say to him!" We watched the whole rescue from our top deck.

Our first port of call was Puntarenas, Costa Rica, meaning "rich coast." The country is known as one of the most fertile spots in all of the Americas. Our bus took us up to the high plateau where the crop is coffee. We bought some coffee for us and as gifts. The growers say they easily compete with Columbian coffee—that the President of Columbia drinks Costa Rican coffee! The main crop on the Atlantic side is bananas, although the country's top cash comes from tourism. It is noteworthy that Costa Rica has more species of birds than all of Canada and the U.S. combined, while their species of butterflies is more than all the Americas combined. In particular, we enjoyed seeing the bright-colored birds, including the great toucan, and butterflies on our jungle walk. We also saw Howler monkeys and the white-faced monkey.

While at sea the next day, we had a big ceremony for everybody crossing the equator, especially the first-timers. It was 4th November, 2001, and we have the certificate signed by the Captain to prove it. Following tradition, Margaret kissed the fish, a 3-foot long fish set up beside the pool for first timers—that is first time across the equator. It was a well-scrubbed specimen! She bought the t-shirt that says, "I kissed the fish!"

Among the ship's crew, the first-timers really got it! They were painted with tomato sauce, sloshed all over with left-over oatmeal, set down on their knees before a Neptune impersonator, "tried" for crimes like keeping the room too clean, and finally thrown into the pool. I swam (in a different pool) as the ship crossed the equator so I could say I swam across the equator. I have a certificate attesting to my feat. What a day! You should see our pictures.

After another day at sea, we landed in Guayaquil, Ecuador, founded by the Spanish in 1527. They gained their independence in 1822, from Spain, after the wars led by Simon Bolivar. These were the same wars that also freed Columbia, Venezuela, and Panama (when it was part of Columbia). The name Ecuador means equator, and of course, the equator runs through the country. The famous Galapagos islands, some 600 miles off the coast, are also owned by Ecuador. The islands are known for the studies done by Charles Darwin in 1835.

We took a "Hacienda" tour out into the country to the banana growers. The banana trees are cut back to the ground each year because the fruit is on new growth each season. The farmers had mesh bags over the growing fruit to keep insects off, or maybe birds. Anyway the huge stalks are brought into a massive processing shed where the bunches are separated, washed, and painted over with a preservative. Then the bananas are boxed in cardboard crates for overseas shipment. We watched the process on a shipment headed for Australia. Lunch was at a lovely colonial hacienda with local costume displays and music: guitars and flute. A large herd of bulls was brought by for us to admire.

Our next stop, after another day on the Pacific, was Callao, Peru. Callao, founded in 1537, was used as the main Spanish port for commerce in the Pacific. Callao is just 20 minutes by car from the capitol, Lima. The port was completely destroyed by an earthquake and the resulting tsunami in 1746.

We took a local plane from Lima to Cusco, which was the ancient Inca capitol. In addition to ruins, Cusco had beautiful cathedrals with unique artwork. The striking story is the Spanish massacre of the Inca warriors at the plaza, or open field, in the valley of Cajamarca. It was November in 1532. Francisco Pizarro and his conquistadors, consisting of 106 foot soldiers and 62 horsemen, slaughtered between six and seven thousand of the Inca men. The Inca fighters with their hand weapons were just helpless against the Spanish muskets. It was about like shooting clay pigeons. So much for the "brave" conquistadors!

Cusco sat on a10,000-foot high plateau. Our guides were worried about our adjustment to the height. They gave us special drinks that were supposed to aid in altitude adjustment. We were ok, but one of our group had to have oxygen and restricted activity. We slept rather uneasily that night.

From Cusco, we took the train up into the Andes mountains to find the remains of an elaborate hidden Inca city near the sharp peak called

Machu Picchu. The train itself was an engineering wonder. It had to come into the station one way, and then back out because the grade was too steep to turn. You could see the spur down below where the train got righted.

It was a beautiful train ride through rugged terrain to get into the back country. You wonder how the Incas could manage in such an out-of-the-way hideaway. They didn't have even the use of wheels! A bus took our group from the train all of the winding steep way to the high Inca town. The site was probably chosen to escape the Spanish conquerors.

The city was on a steep slope that had to be terraced, with stone wall retainers for each terrace. There were hundreds of these terraces around and up to the top. Each terrace had been cultivated with corn and other crops. At the top, and other level places were the stone buildings for residences and meetings. A big central playing field was for players' games and today has grass with the alpacas we saw feeding. Note the ultra fineness of their workmanship. Without any mortar, the stones are laid so close together that you cannot insert a razor blade into the joints.

I have a picture of me standing in front of one stone at the top that is twice my height and over 20 feet across at the bottom. You figure how they quarried and moved these stones without any knowledge of the wheel or any iron tools. The Incas were industrious and amazing workers of their time. They filled a whole room with gold for a ransom of their king from the Spanish. Well, the Spanish executed the king regardless! They couldn't let such a popular figure free to lead an uprising.

We stayed overnight in Cusco after the train ride back. Then we went on to Lima where we caught another bus to go south to Chile. The bus drove through the coastal Atacama Desert, the driest spot on earth. All rain falls on the mountain slopes to the east or blows up and down the ocean coast. The totally barren landscape of Atacama has not had rain in many years! The only humans there are the ones manning the border patrol.

While we enjoyed our two-day three-night stay in Peru, our ship was continuing on down the coast. The ship stopped one night at General

San Martin in Peru, a stop we missed. Then, after a day at sea, the ship put into port at Arica, Chile. Our bus caught up with the ship there, the northern-most port of Chile, next to the border. Arica is the famous export city for the gold and silver mined in Potosi, Bolivia, and brought down on mule back. Potosi is really up the Andes at more than 13,000 feet. The miners who worked for the Spanish conquistadors had a life span of only 10 years because of the poisonous gasses and the air particulate matter in the mines.

That night, out of Arica, the Indonesian crewmembers put on a show of their national singing and dancing. We have a program signed by our table waitress and waiter. Imagine all that talent in the working crew.

Another day at sea, and then we came to Port Coquimbo, Chile. This is one of the best harbors on the coast and is important for fishing, with fish processing plants. Coquimbo means "quiet waters," so named because the harbor is so protected by a peninsula. Everywhere had new and unusual sights.

The very last day of our almost three-week cruise was to the port Valparaiso. Valparaiso, meaning "Valley of Paradise" is the port city for the inland capitol of Chile, Santiago. The port was founded on a large bay in 1536, and lies on many hills that have 16 funiculars to lift the people up the slopes. It's like the San Francisco cable cars, only steeper. Lying on a fault line, the city was destroyed by an earthquake in 1906. Some consider Valparaiso a college town because it has several universities and branches of the University of Chile.

On an inland plain, just two hours from the port, is the capitol, Santiago. This modern city of 5 million people has one-third of the entire population of Chile. We spent several days in Santiago, enjoying the city sights with the view of towering mountains nearby. One day we took a bus trip up a mountain only 45 miles from Santiago to visit the famous ski resort. We were up to the snow line with heavy snow on up to the top although it was summer. The view was spectacular, with the peak on up yet another mile. Their fame is for a world speed record on skis. I've forgotten the exact number, but the record is 200 and some miles per hour!

Watching over the city of Santiago, on a hill 2,800 feet high, is the statue of Madonna, which is comparable to the Christ statue over the city of Rio de Janeiro. How do you conclude such a monumental experience? Words fail me!

We flew out of Santiago back to Miami, Florida. The flight had its own special tale. Somewhere over Peru, the plane had a mechanical problem and turned back to an airport in Chile. It couldn't be allowed to land in an alien country, namely Peru. A part had to be flown in while we waited in a dark, small, vacant airport. After several hours of delay, we did fly on to Florida, arriving hours late. Our plane connection was long gone, so we had to negotiate a different flight home. This flight plan took us to Detroit, then change planes back to BWI! Fortunately the airline realized that missing the connection was not our fault, and didn't charge us for the new arrangement, even though the delay was to a different (Chilean) airline. The good news: we did actually get back home in ok shape!

Each year brings new trips and exciting experiences. In the fall of 2002, we flew to Spain for three weeks of adventure and Elderhostel lectures. The first week was in the capitol, Madrid, with the talks on history and art by professors at the University of Madrid. Our hotel was on the "Puerto Del Sol,"—"Door of the Sun," looking out on beautiful marble buildings with ironwork balconies. A pretty pink façade was just across from our room. The square is similar to the big squares in Washington, D.C., with ample pedestrian space. The oldest building in town was actually given by Egypt and brought over in pieces as a gift for Spain's help in building the Aswan Dam on the Nile. The building, a temple to the sun, is from 2000 B.C.

We actually attended a regular bull fight in the stadium, or circular coliseum, where our group sat in the last row at the very top, a spot chosen by our guide so that we wouldn't concentrate on the blood. Yes, it was bloody, but really very colorful, an entirely new sight. In the parking area outside was a statue to the inventor of penicillin, because antibiotics saved the lives of men gored by bulls.

At the Prado Museum, we saw some of the world's greatest paintings, comparable to the Louvre in Paris.

Another must-see in Madrid was the huge palace of former king Juan Carlos. On a side trip we bussed to Segovia, a town north of Madrid. There we saw a two-tiered set of arches of the Roman aqueduct—over 2000 years old. The Alcazar in town is a former fortress converted into a palace. It was in this town that Isabel was crowned Queen in 1474. She later commissioned Christopher Columbus to sail, and she sold her jewels to finance the ships. Near Segovia, we visited El Escorial, which is the monastery-palace of Spanish monarchs, starting with Philip II. All very impressive.

On a full day trip, we went to Toledo, Spain's first capitol. The "Imperial City" had a Gothic cathedral and two museums devoted to El Greco. The great painter lived and painted in Toledo.

Back in Madrid, we were most pleased to visit a restaurant with dinner and entertainers dancing Tango and Flamenco. Their costumes were extremely elaborate.

South of Madrid, on our way to Granada, we drove through the area of La Mancha. We saw statues everywhere of Cervantes' fictional character Don Quixote. He's the one who tried to lance a windmill. A long bus ride brought us to Granada in southern Spain, and particularly to seeing the nearby Alhambra. Alhambra is a fortified city in itself that was built by the Arabian Muslims, called Moors, when they came across from Africa. The Arabs came into Spain in 511 A.D. and in only 5 years conquered all of the inhabited part of the peninsula. They took advantage of the roads the Romans had built and then abandoned. Then it took the Christians almost 1,000 years to retake the land. The final holdout was the Alhambra, but the caliph finally surrendered because the fortress was isolated from supplies. Queen Isabella negotiated the surrender without a fight in the year 1492, the same year she commissioned Columbus' voyage. The peaceful transition was fortunate because the great art and architecture of Alhambra was preserved. In fact, Isabella and Ferdinand and their court moved into the buildings. Most of the walls, the great mosque, living quarters, palace and other buildings are still there. They are architectural wonders with the inside walls lined in colorful tiles covered in intricate patterns. You have to see this place for yourself! Words can't describe it!

In Granada, meaning "pomegranate," one of our visits was to the Arab silk market. It is well known since medieval times for the finest of silk cloths. On high ground, right in Granada, we had unequalled views of the Alhambra against the background of snow-covered mountains, the Sierra Nevada. Another outing took us to the Cathedral with its exquisite painting and sculpture. In the nearby Capilla Real are the tombs of Ferdinand and Isabella, along with their scepter and jewelry.

Another outing was to La Cartuja monastery, started in 1506. It was under construction for 300 years, exhibiting the Baroque style. Finally we saw the childhood home of Federico Garcia, the famous Spanish poet, playwright, and musician.

Our final week in Spain was in and around Seville, going all the way to the sea. The countryside was covered for miles and miles with orange trees. The river from Seville to the Mediterranean Sea used to be navigable by large ships so that Seville operated as a seaport. Now the shipping comes to the port at the mouth of the river. We were impressed with the size and majesty of the main Cathedral and the mosque. These buildings are covered with irreplaceable art that gives us the highest respect for those who came before. Where is all that talent today? I guess it goes into technology. Art was king in those classical days.

Restaurants and shops had walls covered with tiles showing lovely country scenes. Tile was everywhere. Our hotel in Seville had intricate tile panels on the walls. It was on the Plaza Nueva and directly across from City Hall. Seville has a history spanning 5000 years and claims the cultures of three continents: Africa, Middle East, and Europe, all mixed together. The city motto is "NO 8 Do" or [Seville] does not reject me—in Spanish of course.

The downtown cathedral is the largest Gothic structure anywhere, and is the third largest church in all Christendom. We actually climbed up the ramp up the Giralda, or bell tower. It was smooth with no steps so that a horse could be ridden up—so the rider could ring the bells or issue a call to worship. The belfry at the top is 250 feet high, with stunning views of the river port and giant bells.

Another day, we visited the Fine Arts Museum in the morning and the Alcazar, or royal palace, in the afternoon. Each place is a fine work of art and a joy to see. The next day saw us at the Andalusian school of Equestrian Art, where the show featured world-famous dancing horses. It's hard to believe what those horses do.

At a visit to Cordoba, the feature was the Mezquita or Great Mosque, built between 785 and 987. Three great religions are represented at the site: A Christian Cathedral is built inside of the Mezquita in one of the buildings, a mosque in the other buildings, and then, close by the Jewish quarter. In the Jewish quarter, the great intellectual Maimonides was born.

The next to last evening featured a Flamenco show with brilliantly colored costumes. The men are just as brightly costumed as the women. It's a thrill to watch! On the last day, we bussed to Italica, a Roman suburb just outside of Seville. Roman emperor Trajan gave many favors and support to this place because it was his home town. Amazingly, another Emperor of Rome, Hadrian, was also born in Italica! Also impressive was the Roman amphitheatre and the mosaic floors of the palace ruins from Roman times.

The last night was our farewell banquet get-together before leaving for the Seville airport in the morning. The plane out of Seville crossed the ocean all the way back home. When we arrived home, we could recite the events that we had learned about Spain. Our grandson, David, paid us a nice compliment. He said, "You are a walking history book!"

As usual, this year included many ski trips: one to Copper Mountain, CO with the Behms and Wolfes, another to Seven Springs PA with the Summers, and a separate time with Behms. Usually, once a year, we go to the Kennedy Center in Washington, a bus trip arranged by the Retired Teacher's Association. This year the live show was "Bounce."

My big summer activities were growing vegetables, swimming, and fishing. For 50 years I grew lettuce, tomatoes, beans, Swiss chard, beets, parsley, bell peppers, and rhubarb in my little garden plot. What a pleasure it is to pick fresh greens and bring them in to the table that day! (Actually, it was Margaret who picked the green beans!) We seldom bought tomatoes during the growing season. Almost every warm day I swam in South River at our community beach. That summer was when I caught my biggest fish, a 37 ½ inch, 18 pound rockfish, or technically a stripped bass. That fish earned me a MD State citation. Most of the summer I catch small perch, croaker, spot, and sometimes sea trout. I always enjoy the outing in my boat, even when I get no bites. Recent years have been many more outings of no bites. The main problem now is the modern water pollution.

We escaped the cold in the winter of 2003 by using an RCI exchange to travel to the Dominican Republic for a week in January. The Dominican Republic is the east half of the Caribbean island, while the west half is Haiti. Our half has lush green forest and beautiful countryside. The Haiti side is poor, rather barren, and eroded. The Haitians cut down all their trees and now have the poorest country in the world. See the result of cutting and destroying your environment.

We had a condo with a lovely pool and a very good restaurant by the pool. There was a long path down to the beach on the ocean. The condo provided a small bus, like a golf cart, to drive patrons to the beach for a swim. One day the condo had a beach party with a fish fry at the beach in a little pavilion. I enjoyed some scuba lessons in the pool, and we had a Spanish lesson each day by the pool. Also there were bus trips to sights around the island. We went on one bus trip to a wilderness area. We clambered over rocks to a cave with a deep pool. I swam in the cave water. Another time we were driven to the home of an ex-major league baseball player, a native of the Dominican Republic. He showed off his friendly goats in a sort of performance. Baseball is a big sport there. Apparently many young boys see baseball as the ticket to wealth in the USA. We visited a mahogany forest and watched the local craftsmen work on carving the dark wood. Their artifacts were amazing. I bought a stylized figurine of a woman. It sits on a case in our TV room. The experience was so pleasant that we went back to the same resort the next winter.

After our usual visits to Colorado, Tennessee, and Florida, we took another cruise in September for 11 days, going north out of Baltimore. We sailed with Margaret's Loch Haven Garden Club on Galaxy, of the Celebrity line. The ship was not too big, about 1800 passengers. It sailed down the Chesapeake Bay and then on up to Canada. We stopped in places like Vancouver Island and then up the St. Lawrence River to Quebec. Another stop was in Nova Scotia, where we saw Alexander Graham Bell's estate. He spent a lot of his time there and did significant research. We saw exhibits of his inventions.

I really liked Quebec, especially the old city, down near the dock. We could walk around town from the ship and see the old original buildings. We also visited an enjoyed Arcadia National Park. All of this traveling turns another page in the book of life!

The year 2004 was another big year for us, our 50th wedding anniversary. Margaret planned a full week-long celebration for the entire family in July—even though our real date was November 24. She picked the date so everybody could get here. She had to plan around late school year closing, early school year starts, and cheerleading camp! She worked on the details for six months. We had swimming at Cindy and Greg Behm's, a sightseeing tour of Washington, DC., a trip to the Spy Museum in Washington, D.C., a day at Six Flags amusement park, a morning cruise on the Annapolis Pirate ship, followed by lunch at Buddy's Crab House in Annapolis, an evening ghost tour of old downtown Annapolis, evening theme parties with games, a dinner theatre production of West Side Story, and an afternoon party at church with square dancing. On top of that there was an impromptu Sunday afternoon boat ride. Plus a ghost tour of Annapolis on Sunday evening. Who else could do this much?!

It's hard to list who was here for the week. Margaret got local accommodations for all. Here goes: Behm, Summer, and Wolfe families with all 9 grandchildren, (that's already 17); Dick and Kay Barrans; Kathy Fair with children Michael, Jennifer and Christopher; Ed and Bettie Anne Logan; Melanie Wilkerson with daughters Jamie and Shelby; Pat and Baird Davis; Ginger Wolfe; Randy and Twila Logan with son Ryan; Harry and Barbara Kriede. That's 35, although not all for the whole time. Just try to imagine the food and other arrangements!!

When Thanksgiving and the 24th of November actually came along, we took a Caribbean cruise on Carnival out of Tampa, Florida. Each of our cruises visits different ports. This time, we were at Grand Cayman Island, Cozumel Island, and Mexico. In Mexico we had a bus tour to the Mayan ruins, called Tulum. I was very impressed with the buildings of the Mayans and their orientation. One wall had a slit that was perfectly oriented to allow sunlight all the way into the room only on the winter solstice, 21 December. The Mayans were great astronomers.

On the grounds, we saw native iguanas and many birds. You could see the ocean from the high cliffs at the ruins. I have many pictures of all the sights, and fond memories.

Last February, we had our second trip to the same resort in the Dominican Republic, except that we took different tours around the island. Off hand, I would say that all of our hundreds of trips would be worth a repeat, but we won't live that long!

On the local scene, I give a few sermons at church when our minister is away. Along with teaching an adult Sunday School Class, I also teach a Bible class at the Anne Arundel Detention Center. My main outreach is Evangelism, so I serve as chairman at church and also on our conference Evangelization Committee. We all need to serve wherever possible.

CHAPTER 15

Keeping on Keeping On

As the time flies on, Margaret and I just keep charging along, with new and enlightening experiences every year. There is so much to see and enjoy in God's great creation that one lifetime is just not enough!

In this account, I'm up to the year 2005. We did our usual skiing over the winter in Pennsylvania and Colorado. In Pennsylvania, it was the Behm family and in Colorado with the Norman Wolfe family. In Colorado, we skied on Copper Mountain, one of the nicest areas.

The big trip of the year was our cross-country drive to Arizona to revisit my old stomping ground and my parents' gravesite. The trip took most of the summer—June and July—going in our Odyssey van, and staying many places along the way.

First we stopped in Knoxville, Tennessee and stayed with my cousin Bettie Anne and her husband Ed Logan. While there we also went to see their children: Melanie and husband David, Joellyn and husband John, and Randy Logan with wife Twyla. It is always a very pleasant get-together.

The cross-country drive was similar to the many trips we took with our children back in the 60's and 70's. The hills, forests, and countryside are still there across Tennessee, Arkansas, and Oklahoma. From there, we went North to Kansas and then across to Denver, Colorado. Kansas and eastern Colorado are still pretty flat.

We did extensive hiking in Colorado with Norman and family. Near Denver we, that is, the boys: Norman, Mark, Ryan and I climbed a very rugged steep foothill to a famous eyehole in the top. The climb nearly did me in, but I made it in several hours, toting the camera. The pictures of us standing in this huge eyehole at top are spectacular. The girls stayed behind on the level below. On the return, Norman stayed with me, but the two teenagers got back over an hour ahead. I made a decision: all future hikes will be on the level or a slight grade! Another visit was to Leadville, high in the mountains not very far from Copper Mountain. The small town, started by lead miners, is usually snowed in during winter. It's a step into past history—19th and early 20th century.

Leaving Denver, we drove through the Rockies, both through the Eisenhower tunnel and Vail Pass. The pass above Vail is some 10,000 feet in elevation. It's a dramatic change from the beauty of the mountains to the quite different beauty of the desert as you pass through Grand Junction, Colorado into Utah. Once in Utah, we drove directly to Bryce Canon where we had taken the children back in the 70's.

It was exciting to see again the exotic colors and formations. The bright reds, oranges and whites catch the eye, while the carvings of the winds into cliffs or pillars is thrilling to see. It was so very hot that we had to hike only in the morning, and even then we suffered from heat. Margaret realized she didn't have any head protection and had to stop into the park store for a Bryce logo cap. That cap lasted many years of trips.

I have a picture of Margaret at Sunrise Point, elevation 8015 feet. We not only walked around the rims, but also hiked down a trail into a canyon that ended with "Queen's Garden." Along the way, I have pictures of us in an opening carved through the red rock. My pictures on the computer are worth a look.

Many of the formations have names, such as the maybe 100 foot high pillar called "Queen Victoria." It looks like the queen sitting on a throne. Erosion is continually wearing these formations down so they won't be the same when you get there!

One picture I have is of a beautiful yellow flower that you wouldn't believe could survive on the dry desert soil. Another shows a car road that is cut right through a large orange rock. Some patches have scrub pine and a little grass, but mostly the land is rock and sand.

From Bryce, we drove down to Zion National Park. I have fond memories of water hiking in the river up the narrows with my children years ago. Well, this time, we just hiked as far as the trail went along the side of the river. Actually, there is a shuttle bus in the park that gives you a ride in the valley to various trail heads. I have pictures of snow white flowers growing beside the road, and several pictures of wild turkeys crossing the way. At one place at a cave behind a waterfall, we walked along, looking out at the water cascading over our heads and in front of the view.

Traveling on down through Southern Utah to the Arizona border, we stopped at "Pipe Springs National Monument." It was a home built as a fort to protect locals from the Navaho and Piute Indians. The whole place belonged to the Mormon church, and a family, under the direction of Brigham Young, was assigned for a designated period of time to occupy the building and represent the church. The family collected the required tithes from the local Mormon ranchers. The tithe was paid in heads of cattle and in milk, which the family processed into cheese for transport.

After crossing into Arizona, we came to the Navajo Bridge over the Colorado River. The river is small here, and not very impressive but, the neat thing was that a new car bridge had been built along side of the old bridge, which is now used only for walking and picture taking. We walked across for the view. You should see my pictures of the green water!

Later, at the rim of the Grand Canyon, I have more scenes of the great river and its gorge. The roads in Grand Canyon Park were so crowded that we could hardly find a parking place, or a stopping place for pictures. But we did manage a few photos overlooking the great canyon. Finally down in Tucson in southern Arizona, we visited the Davis Family, Pat and Baird Davis. Pat is a daughter of Sheldon Wolfe, my father's younger brother. We stayed in a condo in downtown Tucson, and visited in their lovely home in the foothills of the Catalina Mountains overlooking the city of Tucson. It was a memory lane for me to see again my parents' home right there on Florence Drive, facing the Catalina mountains. We drove by the house very slowly, and one of the occupants came out. We met the elderly gentleman and his daughter who have been living there many years, and had a wonderful chat with them. We still get a Christmas card from them.

Finally, the main object of our trip, was finding my parents' grave on the north side of Tucson. We had difficulty finding the cemetery because it had changed names since my parents' burial. And in the blazing hot sun, the half submerged marker was hard to spot. However, the stone marker with "WOLFE" and my parents' names along with dates was ok. Missing was the brass cylinder for flowers. I got the management to give me a new brass container and filled it with new flowers—artificial ones of course. Real flowers wouldn't last a day out there. Those red roses will last a year or more until management throws them out. Of course, it's time for me to go again.

We also wandered around the campus of University of Arizona, which Carvel graduated from. And we spent a pleasant afternoon checking out the local flowers in a small nature park.

We drove from Tucson to Branson Missouri. We were there for three days and saw a number of shows, including one on a dinner-boat ride. We were pleased to be able to purchase tickets to the shows immediately.

We drove from there to Margaret's cousin Margaret King in Piedmont, Missouri. She is the daughter of Margaret's aunt on her father's side. She and husband Joe showed us the Owens cemetery there, and we got to see a birthday party for her granddaughter. From there we drove safely home. I believe the dear Lord watches over us since we seem to arrive home safely from all these trips.

In the fall, October 2005, we returned to Tennessee for the wedding of Leah, daughter of Joellyn and John Buchanan, and thus granddaughter of Bettie Anne Logan, to Abel Cushing. It was a lovely wedding with all the trimmings. I believe the couple now lives in Indiana.

Year 2006 was another year that was full, as usual, of invigorating events and trips. We attended three graduations in our family around the country. David Behm graduated from Bridgewater College in Virginia, near Staunton in the Shenandoah Valley, west of the Blue

Ridge mountains. David is the oldest of the three sons of my daughter, Cynthia. His younger bother, Gary Behm, graduated from high school in Westminster, MD. Then my son Norman Wolfe's daughter, Cara Wolfe, graduated from high school in Denver, Colorado. We enjoyed the pomp and ceremony, and managed to sit through all the speeches. Of course the two high school graduates went off to college in the fall.

Our ski trips were many and widespread. Over Christmas '05, we took Eileen Summers' family from Florida skiing on Shawnee Mountain, PA, for a three-day holiday weekend. Finally, we had our usual ski week in Colorado at Beaver Creek with Norman Wolfe family. All the trips had great snow on the mountain and we had fun together. The top at Beaver Creek is over 10,000 feet high.

In the early summer, we exchanged with RCI for a condo on Treasure Island, just off from St. Petersburg on the Florida Gulf coast. It is a timeshare unit that we get by trading our unit in Ocean City, MD. The Summers came to our place for part of the week, and we just had a good time on the beach and in the gulf. I love swimming all the time, especially in the Gulf, and try to get a unit there every year in May or early June.

Our square dancing clubs have conventions every year for a three-day marathon of dancing. This year, one was in Virginia near Washington, and another at Hunt Valley near Timonium, MD. We attended both for a lot of fun and a vigorous time of dancing, both square and round dancing. My summer is mostly a lot of swimming, boating, fishing, and Bible Study. I really enjoy teaching Bible at the local prison because the inmates are to eager to grasp all they can.

Our major trip in 06 was in the fall to New Zealand and Australia. In late October, we flew from L. A. directly to Auckland, New Zealand, passing the International Date Line. There was much to see in Auckland, along with the lectures on the history and culture of the two islands. Auckland is on the North Island and is a major seaport. We visited the gorgeous gardens of "Eden" and also the museum with the "Maori" culture. The Maori, meaning "ordinary," were the native tribes living on the island when it was first explored by the Dutch seaman, Abel Tasman in 1642. Captain Cook made it there over 100 years later. Auckland is

157

shaped by 49 volcanoes in the immediate area. They are now inactive and I have pictures from the top of one overlooking the city.

On the bus ride south to Rotorua, we stopped at the Kiwi House to see the famous native bird found only in New Zealand. Because kiwis are nocturnal, the viewing room was kept dark. To avoid overstressing the kiwis, only one at a time was nudged into the viewing area. The director showed us x-rays of a kiwi with its single egg almost as large as the bird's small body.

Another stop was at the Waitomo Caves to see the glow worms. We had a boat ride through the caves and at one point the worms dangled from the arched ceiling in long stringers. They glow to attract insects, which are their food.

On the rugged west coast, there were thousands of gulls on huge rocks. It is a rookery. Also, a familiar sight to those who have been to our Yellowstone Park, was the area of hot springs and geysers. We watched a number of the geysers erupt just like in Yellowstone. Do see my pictures!

At Te Puia, a Maori reservation, we had dinner in a large tent, and watched elaborate dances and music put on by the Maori people, wearing native costumes. Their skin was carefully painted in fine designs.

From the North Island, we flew to Christchurch on the south Island. That town is the departure point for those flying to Antarctica, since it is the closest air facility. My son, Norman, flew out of Christchurch each time he deployed to McMurdo Sound and the South Pole. We toured Lake Tednau, one of the largest mountain lakes on our bus, which drove slowly through steep passes to Fiordland and Milford Sound. The tops of the mountains still had snow and in season, the skiing was said to be great. A very exciting boat ride was on Milford Sound, down the deep fiord. Along the way, you could see high water falls and seals basking on the rocks. It is a wonderland!

Another cruise boat took us across lake Wakatipu to a sheep farm. At the farm, we watched a pro sheer an entire sheep in just a few minutes. That's sight! Your tour guide, who runs a sheep farm, thought the operation was too slow, but instructive for tourists. As in Wales, there are more sheep on the island than people.

The last day of October, lunch was at the Skyline Restaurant, with access by a mountain gondola both ways. The ride was fun, unless one had fear of heights, and the view was spectacular at the restaurant. Then our coach took us on to the hotel in Queenstown. From Queenstown, we flew back to Christchurch. This time we enjoyed the exhibits of penguins at the Antarctic Center. There were wild penguins on our boat trip in Milford Sound, but here we saw captive ones. We enjoyed trying on the heavy parka and clothes, which are worn at the pole. I have a picture of Margaret in an Antarctic parka—only her nose is visible. Margaret bought a t-shirt with the Antarctic logo, and we took pictures in front of the penguin exhibits.

From Christchurch, we flew into Sydney, Australia, the first of November. Australia is so big that it is a continent instead of an island. Sydney is the main port and largest city with a population of 4 million. We really enjoyed the several days in Sydney with all the parks featuring flora and fauna, as well as its modern buildings with the famous Opera House. Sydney started out as a penal colony for the British and is now a very cosmopolitan city.

We visited the local zoo, especially enjoying the koala bears, the kangaroos, the dingo (dog) and the great variety of birds. One store showed a mine (a simulated example) for extracting opals, and exhibited the beautiful opal jewelry. In the evening we went to the opera house on the harbor and saw a top notch performance of "The Pirates of Penzance." It was very interesting to see the show after we had walked through the empty building that afternoon just to take in the unique architecture. At Darling Harbor, which was one block from our hotel, we walked through the aquarium, on our free time, seeing the most colorful fish. I actually bought a typical Australian sun hat, all leather, in a market in town—one of my very few purchases.

We then flew from Sydney to Alice Springs in the center of the continent and also in the middle of the vast desert. The aborigines got here first and have lived in the area for 15 thousand years. They still create arts and crafts for the many visitors. Among our many lectures on the area was one on a field trip to the Royal Flying Doctor Service. The doctors fly in to provide health care to the Outback, as scheduled, and then fly back.

One evening we bussed to Ooraminna Bush Camp for a ranch dinner and a talk on the cattle business. Ranching is a precise science. The cattle roam over a huge area, some 100 acres per head, and come back to an enclosed place every few days for water. The deep well and resulting water hole is a necessity for the cattle to live. Now, most of the season, the gates are open so the cattle can walk through. At round up time, the ranchers close the exit gate so over a period of a few days all head are caught in the enclosure. Then the market truck merely walks them into the truck. This clever scheme minimizes the number of cowhands required, and one family, in our case, the Hayes, can handle the whole ranch—over a hundred thousand acres.

We took a number of field trips out of Alice Springs, the week we were there. Trips were to Simpson's Gap, Stanley Chasm, the Olive Pink Botanical Garden, and one evening to the Musical Heritage for the music with costumes of the aborigines. Departing from Alice Springs, our bus took us to Uluru, which is the famous Ayers Rock. The English named it Ayers Rock, but the native designation, which has been revived, is Uluru. On the way, we stopped at a camel farm. Camels were originally brought to Australia for carrying building materials to the railroad. When the railroad was finished, the workers simply left the camels. The camels flourished, and now large herds roam the wild lands, eating fodder that the native kangaroos should be eating. Occasional roundups collect the camels to reduce their numbers. At this farm some camels were penned up for tourists to see.

Ayers Rock is the largest free-standing rock in the world. It is several miles long and some hundreds of feet high. We circled the rock on our bus and walked to it at one point. It is a barren, sandy colored chunk. The rock is sacred to the local aborigines, and so no one is allowed to climb on the rock. It is quite impressive, but you won't guess the principal attraction. In the evening, we departed from our digs at the Culture Center, to return to a special viewing area on the west side of the mountain, about one mile away. To our astonishment, there were in place several dozen other busses at the site. A regular traffic jam in nowhere. Margaret was fuming about everyone sitting on camp stools staring at a rock, which obviously wasn't going anywhere! It was getting late, and the sun was low, while I took some pictures and just wondered why everybody was there. After all, we had just seen the whole rock earlier in the day. Then it happened! As the sun neared the horizon, this huge red rock started to change color. The red faded into a gold, and then shone brilliantly in a glowing bright gold. It was shimmering and iridescent in reflected light. I rate it as the most stunning sight that I've seen, absolutely incomparable! You must see my pictures to get a tiny idea of the spectacle.

The next day, we flew from Ayers Rock airport to the city Cairns (pronounced Cans) in tropical North Queensland. Cairns is on the north coast and in a tropical rainforest, the opposite of that dry desert inland. What a contrast to go from the deep desert to the lush tropics. It's comparable to going between Key West and southern Arizona.

As usual, we had field trips out of Cairns to the surrounding area. First we went to nearby Kuranda and visited the Butterfly Sanctuary. They had an enclosed area with hundreds of exotic butterflies flying among the plants. There were displays of mounted butterflies from all over the world. Then we went on a Sky Rail ride over the top of a vast rainforest. The sky ride is sort of like a small gondola on a high cable that carried us up over the tops of 150-foot trees. There were various stations along the way where one could get off for a better view of the lush vegetation and then hop on another car. We saw fig trees, giant Red Pender trees, oak, mistletoe, along with parasitic flowers like orchids, and innumerable birds. Down underneath the canopy were rivers with falls and in the water, not seen, were fresh water crocodiles, tortoises, and water birds. The Sky Rail took us all the way to another town, Caravonica, where we caught the bus back to our hotel.

Another day, we took a boat cruise out to the Great Barrier Reef for a full day on the water. I believe it is the largest reef, going for hundreds of miles along the northern coast of Australia. At several places, the boat anchored for us to go snorkeling over the coral to view exotic fish. I bought an underwater camera for he purpose, and took a couple dozen pictures. In general my pictures are cloudy as I couldn't get close enough to the bottom. However, you can see the coral formations, some fish and a giant clam, which was open while breathing. The brain coral are prominent along with coral fingers flowing in the current. It was a memorable experience, despite the quality of my pictures.

While still at Cairns, we had a day trip to the Rainforest Habitat Centre with a guided walk. We saw up close: koalas (asleep in the daytime), kangaroos, bouncing languidly along, crocodiles, wallabies, and aviaries of birds. One of the largest birds is the Southern Cassowary, which grows to 8 feet tall and is very aggressive. Give it plenty of space! I have a picture of me next to a green and red parrot, with another parrot, red, blue, and black, nearby.

A large tree, occupying an entire city park right across the street from our city hotel, held hundreds of sleeping bats all day. The largest bat, called the flying fox, has a wingspan of 4 feet. You just have to be there to appreciate the variety of animals created by God.

All good things, even 15 thousand miles from home, come to an end. We flew from Cairns back to Sydney, then across the date line, all the way back to LA. Of course, we got back the day we had lost going west. Then, the last flight, coast to coast, took us to Baltimore. You can imagine how tired we were by the time we arrived at home! Would I do it again? By all means!

Now we are up to the year 2007 with new trips and many old repeat activities. Winter ski trips were again local and in Colorado. I do the blue slopes and some of the black diamond slopes. My preference is definitely on the groomed slopes.

For square and round dancing, we go to several local clubs along with three conventions. The conventions were: March—in northern Virginia; July—in Hunt Valley, MD, and September—in Chincoteague, Virginia. The dances include bolero, two-step, waltz, jive, cha-cha, rumba, fox trot, and tango.

Our out-of-country trip was a Caribbean cruise in June. The cruise helped celebrate my birthday on 11 June, and followed a week on the beach at St. Petersburg, Florida. The cruise visited a number of islands along with the countries of Mexico and Belize. The Summers family joined us on the boat, so we had a grand time together. We seldom saw Kevin because he stayed with the teenage group organized by the Carnival cruise directors.

In Mexico, there with a tour with a long bus ride to the Mayan ruins. I was impressed with the many-stepped pyramid in the center of the Mayan City. The pyramid had a small enclosure on the flat top that was apparently used for sacrifices. There were the remains of many other buildings along with parts of the city wall and gates. One building was oriented with an opening that showed the sun on the winter solstice. Their grasp of astronomy was similar to the ability of the Incas at Machu Pichu. From the top of the cliff, we could see the water in the Caribbean and a small beach. In addition to the ruins, I have pictures of the native iguana.

A very unusual trip was the tubing in Belize. We hiked through tropical jungle for a mile in our swimsuits and water shoes to a river access. There, they gave each of us a big inner tube to climb into in the water. The water was shallow, only a foot or so deep, and had places where the tube caught on the bottom. Many people had to get up and walk across sand bars to find deeper water. The guide said the water was low that year. However, the guide took Margaret and me under his wing. He guided us through the deepest parts of the river by having Margaret hook her feet under his tube, and me hooking my feet under her tube. He paddled and we paddled. We never got up out of our tube the whole ride. About a mile of the long ride was in a tunnel through the mountain. We could see live bats on the ceiling along with stalactites hanging down. It was an exciting sight and so different from the tours elsewhere.

Other attractions on the cruise were snorkeling over reefs and on a sand bar in waist-deep water, playing with stingrays. We all petted the rays and stroked the under-side as guides flipped them over. Actually, they were very smooth with no scales.

In June, we flew out to Denver again. This time was for Mark's high school graduation. It was easy compared to last year when we attended 4 graduations. It's a job to keep up with our family of 9 grandchildren. The Lord has blessed us. They are all wonderfully nice and intelligent.

The winter of 2008 was hard on Margaret as she made four trips on an emergency basis to California to visit her sister, Elizabeth. Elizabeth was in failing health and died on 7 March. Margaret took care of all the arrangements and had her sister's ashes put next to their parents' at Forest Lawn Cemetery in Glendale, CA. [Margaret remarks: The process was especially trying because it seemed that everything that could go wrong did. First, I had made contracts with a funeral home and Forest Lawn cemetery before I left California, thinking, however, that Elizabeth was doing well and would be getting physical therapy. Elizabeth died while I was on the plane coming home. The first problem was that no doctor would issue a death certificate, so the funeral home couldn't collect her body and cremate. The funeral home tried for about a week to find some doctor who would sign papers for her. Finally the hospice doctor signed, even though I had just removed her from hospice. Then, the funeral home couldn't come up with the contract that I had signed. Fortunately, my neighbor let me fax papers. Then the cemetery said that they didn't have the papers for her niche. Fax again. Then they said the niche which had been sold to me was already occupied. Fax again. Finally all was settled. Except for filing the year's income taxes. She had signed the federal forms while I was there, so they were possible. The state forms were trickier, but later sent in.]

Our usual ski trips to Seven Springs and to Colorado still happened with some great skiing.

The big trip over the summer was to the Black Sea. We cruised on an Oceania ship from Istanbul (old Constantinople) Turkey to: Nessebur, Bulgaria; Constanta, Romania; Odessa, Ukraine; Sevastopol, Ukraine, Yalta, Crimean Peninsula; Sochi, Russia; and on down the cost of Turkey to Kusadasi near Ephesus. This was a top notch cruise with so many new places to experience.

Istanbul, which I call by its former name Constantinople, is just a different world from us. The first unusual event was our admittance to the over a 1000 year-old Sultan's palace. This palace was the main tourist sight in town. It's open every day except Tuesday, and of course, Tuesday is the day we had been assigned to visit the city. At first it was announced that visitors would miss the palace, and most did. Our Oceania Cruise ship group of about two bus loads, was given a special showing just for us. We were escorted through the lavishly decorated rooms and the outside plazas as a private, casual tour. When we got to our ship, we spoke to others who had come a day early just to see the palace. They had had to put up with thousands of tourists in a real mob scene!

We took off our shoes to walk into the blue mosque—a huge building with lovely Persian rugs for the men there for prayers. The outside has a blue tile roof, giving it its name, and tall, tall minarets on the corners.

We also walked through a shopping area with brightly painted vaulted ceilings. In eye stopping window displays, there were carved plates of silver, many of gold, and highly painted porcelain. The local women particularly prized gold—personal ornaments—because it was the only way they could store wealth. Women were not allowed to have business ventures or inherit money. How would you like to live there?

[Margaret interjects: Carvel was so excited here that he was taking pictures of the mosque as he walked over the cobble stone street from the bus to the curb. He hurried to avoid an oncoming bus, tripped and fell. Since his camera was in hand and he wanted to protect it, he went down on his left elbow. That was a mistake. He saved the camera, but tore the skin on the lower arm to the elbow. We were contending with blood all morning long. The poor tour guide didn't have any first aid ointments or band aids with her. We daubed with Kleenex and later with paper towels. When we returned to the ship, I insisted that he see the ship's doctor. The doctor was a tall blond from Sweden, and he looked like he hadn't had a patient for weeks. He was delighted to see us and proceeded to sew up Carvel's arm and thoroughly bandage it. The next morning the ship officer slipped the bill under our door. We couldn't imagine it! He charged $150 for an office visit, another $105 for consultation, and then for the disinfectant, stitches, bandages, and goodness knows what else. He ran up a bill of $750!

Of course we had to pay it—the ship has our credit card! The good news is that after we returned home and submitted the bill to our insurance—Blue Cross—Blue Shield—they reimbursed us.] I thought sure, being out of the country, that the bill was on me. Even though my arm healed during the long cruise, I never went back to that doctor. I didn't want to find out how many hundred it would be to take the stitches out. I let Margaret take them out back at home.

The Oceania cruise ship was elegant with nice cabins and outdoor verandas for each cabin. We enjoyed the ship and wonderful six star dinners.

Our first port after we left Istanbul was in Bulgaria at Nessebur on the Black Sea. We toured old chapels going all the way back to the beginning of Christianity in that area. Our bus took the group out into the countryside to a planned tourist center. It consisted of many shops with craftsmen and a large pavilion for wine tasting. We were met at the gate by a young girl in a bright local dress handing out a welcome snack. At the silver shop, Margaret bought a crafted, engraved bracelet directly from the maker. I have a picture of the engraver who made Margaret's bracelet. It is a high quality silver with much higher purity than the Mexican silver found over here. Since the main point of the stop was a wine tasting experience, (and to sell wine from the wine tasting) we made all the folks at our table extra happy as they got to sip the wine samples offered to us! Actually, I think many of the tourists did buy wine from the winery.

Our next port was Constanta in Romania, the city that is closest to where the Danube River empties into the Black Sea. River cruises across Europe end up at Constanta. We toured ancient ruins that date back to the Greek settlement near 500 B.C. In 29 B.C. the area was conquered by the Romans and named "Tomis." You see marks and remains from almost all periods of history! A real treat was the dance put on by a local group dressed in their handmade gorgeous costumes. [Margaret remarks about the historical ruins: It was the story all around the Black Sea: The Greeks were here, the Romans were here, the Bulgarians were here, the Ottoman Empire was here, the Russians were here, the Germans were here . . . with a few variations.]

Next, we stopped at Odessa in the Ukraine, the largest port on the Black Sea. Again the history goes back to the ancient Greeks. It's amazing all the cultures involved in such a cosmopolitan city from the Greeks, the Crimean Tatars, the Bulgarians, the Ottoman Turks, up to the Russians who made it a naval base in 1794. Under Catherine the Great, Odessa became the capitol of New Russia. I was particularly impressed with the staircase which leads down from very wide Primorsky Boulevard to the water below—192 full steps. Some call Odessa the Riviera of the Black Sea.

A second stop in the country of Ukraine was at Sevastopol, which translated from the Greek means "majestic city." It is known as a "hero city" because of its valiant stand against the Nazis in World War II. We toured the city and ancient ruins along the coast, all memorable sights.

After a day at sea, we put into Sochi, Russia, our first step into the country of Russia. As a matter of fact, all the countries along the Black Sea marked our first visit. Sochi is primarily known in Russia as a destination resort, with mild summer beaches on the sea, looking at the snow-covered peaks of the Caucasus. In 2014 the winter Olympics will be held in those mountains overlooking Sochi. Tennis stars like Maria Sharapova trained and lived here. Even Joseph Stalin had his summer home, "dacha," built here. We visited one of the palaces which had survived the Communist regime as a tuberculosis sanitarium. We also saw a Botanical Gardens and a tea plantation.

Our final stop on the Black Sea was back on the Crimean peninsula at the famous Yalta. Yalta began as a Greek colony, later a Byzantine port, then a part of the Ottoman Empire, and finally a part of Russia through the Russo-Turkish War of 1787-1792. It is not a part of the Ukraine, although most of its people are Russian, and they consider it a Russian resort. Writer Leo Tolstoy spent summers here and the Tsars built their summer homes there. It was Tsar Nicholas II who built the Livadia Palace in 1911. It was there in the Livadia Palace in 1945 that the "Big Three" powers held the Yalta Conference to decide the future of Germany. The three leaders were Franklin Delano Roosevelt for the U.S., Winston Churchill for England, and Joseph Stalin for the USSR. I walked around the conference room and looked at each chair where each of those Heads of State sat. The chairs are still in their original spot!

This conference decided to form our United Nations, which is still going strong! The guide told us that each of the leaders had a fancy palace to stay in, except Roosevelt, who had quarters right there in the back rooms. This was a concession to his paralysis (from polio) which confined him to a wheel chair.

[Margaret adds: Everywhere we went, I asked the guide why the sea was called "the Black Sea," and if it was so called today. I heard that the Greeks called it "The Friendly Sea," apparently in an effort to placate the evil spirits there. But since that time it had been Black in every era. Every guide had a different answer to the why of the name. One answer was that so many sailors died navigating it that it caused widows to have to wear black. Another was that at one place reeds grew close to the surface and made the water look black. Another was the corroding ship bottoms—due to high sulfur content—turned the water and ship hulls black. Another was that the poet Ovid was banished from Rome for writing sex revelations about Octavia, the empress. He hated Constanta, his residence in exile, and wrote about the black sea surrounding him. Maybe that last was the major reason.]

Out of Yalta there were two days of cruising down to the port Kusadasi on the Turkey coast. We sailed through the narrows and the Dardanelles that connect the Black Sea with the Mediterranean Sea (or rather that neck called the Aegean Sea). Kusadasi, on the coast, is a major tourist center and a resort with its hot summers following mild winters. Ephesus is just a 20-minute bus ride inland up river. What you don't see is that the river has filled in the land for several miles between the two cities. In St Paul's time (40-60 AD) Ephesus was the port city on the sea. The magnitude of coastal changes is amazing. Of course, Ephesus is the main attraction with its well-preserved ruins, the ancient library and the great amphitheater. The many tiers of stone benches are still there to the top. They held thousands of spectators. I stood where Paul must have stood, on the platform in front of the great crowd that came to hear Paul speak. It was so thrilling just to be there with your imagination running wild in history! On the side, part way up the hill, were the toilets—in a small building—just holes in the stone bench, rather close together for conversation.

The two-story library of Celsus has been restored. The original, from Roman times, was burned and lost thousands of precious scrolls, many irreplaceable. It had rivaled the library in Alexandria, Egypt. The librarians pioneered the use of parchment for scrolls when rival Egypt refused to export their papyrus, made from Nile River reeds. Think what a loss of our history and literature! We were informed of the reason that the ancient part of the city is so well-preserved today. The nearby river with its swamp bred mosquitoes that caused a malaria epidemic. The population from Roman times simply moved elsewhere, leaving the city intact. Notice that some good comes out of bad.

Back in Kusadasi, we visited a Persian rug shop with an elaborate showing of hand made rugs. Guess what happened? We actually bought a beautifully woven rug with attractive design. It wasn't cheap—close to $2000. I think it is a real treasure to have that lovely showpiece in front of our living room fireplace. Some things are worth the extra price. By the way, Kusadasi means "bird island." There is a Pigeon Island nearby.

From the Turkish coast, we sailed to the Greek Island, Santorini, the most beautiful of the Greek Islands. It is a spectacle you must see as words of description are just insufficient! We off loaded into a small ship, which landed us on the side of the island which was supposedly easier to climb than the side near the ship anchorage. However, the climb had us all huffing and puffing. Then we walked around the narrow passageways between tiny white buildings to view the steep side of the island. From the top you could see a ring of islands in a circle around the sea, which was actually a caldera. This sunken caldera, now 1300 feet deep, was once a volcano. An extremely big eruption happened before 1000 B.C. This eruption is believed to have destroyed the Minoan civilization on Santorini and neighboring islands. Some think that this eruption was the source of some of the plagues described in the Bible, such as turning the Nile River red, which occurred during the time of Moses in Egypt. The eruption was at about that time!

Finally, we rode a funicular on a cable down the cliff to the shore below. From there a tender took us to our ship. The next day, after an overnight ride, we docked at the port Piraeus near Athens Greece. Our return flight from Athens airport went all the way to New York. As you can see, we live for adventure and enjoy every minute of it!

Carvel & Margaret, 2009

CHAPTER 16

A New Beginning

You wouldn't guess that at our age, over 80, we are starting anew at another home. After 51 years and raising a family in the same house, we moved to another house. The new place is still in Loch Haven and just across the street from the previous home. We are slightly up the hill and on the water side of the community. I now have my own beach, an nice pier with a boat lift, and a magnificent view across our inlet and on across the South River. The house was extensively remodeled about 10 years earlier and has excellent décor. It is larger than our previous house with two stories and so much more floor space. The property includes a two-car garage, a large deck on both levels, a shed for tools, and a boardwalk with railing down to the pier. I'm delighted to have a place on the water for my boat. Also, I do swimming, crabbing and fishing right here at home. Of course, better fishing is by boat out to the Chesapeake Bay.

[Margaret notes: The impetus for buying the new home was that Carvel couldn't beg or rent boat docking in Loch Haven. He had kept the boat at Dick Edward's pier for some 45 years. But Dick died, so the pier wasn't available when that house was resold. Then he kept it at Rosalie Creighton's, but she decided not to continue the arrangement after a year. Then he had it at the pier of a friend, Grace and Art Romer, but after three years, they moved and sold. The house at 3538 was on the market. Carvel asked me if I could be satisfied living in the house. Cindy and I walked up and peeked in the windows and agreed that the house seemed very nice. Actually we didn't realize how large or how nice it was from just looking in the windows. Later in the week, we walked up to the house, knocked, visited with Don Knotts, the owner, and made him an offer. The final arrangements came through a real estate agent. We definitely bought a pier that had a house attached! It was a house that had been built some 50 years before. Because the original house was small, the additions make for some odd architectural spaces, including what was probably a big downer on sales—a circular staircase to the downstairs. At first I thought the stairs would be a problem, but we have gone up and down so many times, that they present no difficulty at all.]

We moved into the new digs in November 2009 and have done a lot since. Margaret insisted on a third bathroom—a second downstairs. We are on a slope so the upstairs is at ground level out front, and the downstairs is at ground level out back. Also, we are at least 25 feet above the river, so there is no concern about a tidal surge. The new bath is the latest in hardware and convenience. All the pieces are in a gold finish, and the shower room has THREE shower heads. I really enjoy that shower. Upstairs, we put in a new washer and dryer so laundry could stay upstairs. There already was a laundry room with washer and dryer downstairs. The connecting stairs are a tight circle like a fireman's well, so you wouldn't want to carry much up and down. One upstairs room, billed as a bedroom, has been converted into a computer room with writing desks. The entire interior was painted white, which we have not changed. Swag curtains and/or blinds decorated all the windows, and we have enjoyed them. The floors were mostly hardwood upstairs and carpeted downstairs. None of the carpets needed replacement.

The outside has also undergone major renovation. I cut out some three dozen young trees and heavy brush on both sides of the property. Now opened up, the mountain laurel are blooming profusely, the holly have berries, and daffodils have poked through. It looks good with an ivy ground cover. Margaret went to war on the Virginia creeper, which was overrunning everything, and she won the battle. We also have beautiful flower beds out front and out back, along with azaleas and rhododendrons.

Between jobs at home, we had ample outings all year in 2009. In January and February, we had our skiing at Seven Springs and out in Beaver Creek. May saw us back in Denver for Mark Wolfe's graduation from a junior college. Then the next month, we had a week on the beach at Treasure Island, just off of Saint Petersburg, Florida. We also bought a new van, a Honda Odyssey, the same year as the new house. It's nice to have the money for these without any future payments. That's the result of saving and investing all your life!

The major trip came in September on a cruise through the Panama Canal. We flew to San Diego and visited several days with the senior Behms, Tom and wife Sel. Tom is the father of Greg, our daughter Cynthia's husband. It was very pleasant to see the local sights and visit the well-known zoo. I have pictures of all the exotic animals at the San Diego Zoo.

At the port, we boarded the ship Statendam of Holland America. Sailing with us, in the next door cabin, were Kay, my first cousin, and her husband Dick Barrans. She was fulfilling her long-held desire to go through the Panama Canal. Our first stop in Mexico was Puerto Vallarta, where we swam with the local dolphins in a large swimming pool. I held onto the dorsal fin while the dolphin swam around the pool at a high speed. That was fun!

After a day at sea, our next port was Huatulco in Mexico. Our land tour included a bird sanctuary. Actually, our walk was through the jungle where the colorful birds lived in the wild.

A day later we visited the port of Puerto Chiapas, also in Mexico. The locals put on a terrific dancing display in their colorful handmade costumes. There were about 10 couples that danced together and then some dances of men only or women only. I have the pictures. Then we took a bus tour to Mayan ruins. The archaelogical site was called Izapa. An old stone wall surrounded a large grass, level field which was apparently used for games, like kicking a unique homemade ball. A church in town displayed a half-dozen girls in very elaborate dresses.

From there, we cruised overnight to Guatemala and spent the day in Puerto Quetzal. We mostly walked around town on the old cobblestone streets. The old architecture, especially the churches, was very dramatic.

Another overnight cruise brought us to Corinto, Nicaragua, where we bussed up into nearby hills to the thermal area with hot springs. There were many bubbling mud pots and steaming pools. It certainly reminded me of our Yellowstone National Park. You can see the rising steam in my pictures. Other places than home have these natural wonders!

The Barrans did not go with us on these land trips because Dick was too weak for much walking. However, they took various bus trips, which were less strenuous. We always met up for breakfast in the morning, dinner in the evening, and the evening show.

The next day and night we spent at sea before arriving in the morning at Fuerte Amador in Panama. This, of course, is on the Pacific side of the Panama Canal near the capitol city called Panama City. We toured the old Spanish fort called Amador and then took a buzz around Panama City. Unfortunately, the main attraction to me was the church of the golden altar, which was closed. I remembered that church from the time I spent stationed there in the army. The entire front of the church, floor to ceiling, side to side, was covered with gold. The gold was saved from the Spanish by being painted white during the occupation. So after bragging about the building, I couldn't show it to my cousin Kay, who was with us.

A day later, our 12th day out, we entered the Panama Canal for our crossing. This was my first time of actually seeing the canal and its locks. On the Pacific side we were raised up by three locks called Miraflores locks. Each lock raised the boat some 50 feet to get up to Gatun Lake. It was a sight to see the huge gates swing open to each side. The locks are so perfectly balanced that they open and close with little power. Then after the ship was inside and the gates closed, the water flowed in from the higher level—all by gravity flow. Our ship only had a couple of feet clearance on each side. When the water level in a lock was equal to the next compartment, the gate ahead opened and the ship moved out. Actually the ship was pulled by railcars on the side. The major part of the crossing was in Gatun Lake. This lake was created by dams to control the river water. The river periodically floods, and had to be harnessed to provide water for the canal. It is water from the lake that is used in each lock and flows down to the sea. This enormous amount of water must be replaced by the local rainfall and adjacent rivers. It's important that Panama has one of the largest annual rainfalls. The rain comes every day, usually in the afternoon. I used to say, when I lived there, that I could tell time by the rain. It came every day just one hour later than the previous day.

Gatun Lake is lined with dense jungles and has islands, which are near primal and uninhabited. I had a walk across one of he islands when I was stationed in Panama—to see exotic animals such as monkeys and insects—some ants an inch long. Our ship passed under several large suspension bridges, in particular the international bridge that connects North America with South America. We also saw the digging on one side to eventually put in another, larger, canal to handle the larger ships of today—aircraft carriers and oil tankers.

It rained in the afternoon as we traveled the three locks down to the sea level on the Atlantic or Caribbean side. I didn't get many pictures on that side. Of course, each lock lowered the ship some 50 feet, as the water flowed out and down to the next level. The locks are an engineering marvel and still over 100 years after construction (about 1910) they work just fine. It's interesting to note that the canal generally goes North-South because of the hook of land connecting North to South America.

We sailed right out of the bay, next to the city of Cristobal, on the Caribbean coast of Panama, and on down to Cartagena in Colombia. We arrived in Cartagena the next morning and had our last day on land. On our tour of the city, we viewed a beautiful cathedral, homes with flower covered balconies, and an old Spanish fort. From surrounding hills, there was a sparkling panorama of the whole port.

From Columbia, we sailed a full two days back to Fort Lauderdale, Florida and from there we flew on home. The days on the ship were quite enjoyable. I swam in the pool each day, played some miniature golf, and shuffleboard. A big attraction is the gourmet meals at each of the dining facilities. Everyone should see the Canal, a real contribution to the world from the United States, and enjoy the weeks at sea.

Before the year was over, we enjoyed two small out-of-town trips. One was to the Catoctin Mountains for viewing the fall colors. We were just outside of the secret location of Camp David—the private camp the government maintains for the presidents. The other trip was three days in New York to see the Statue of Liberty and Broadway shows. We also saw the barren area left after the Twin Towers came down in 9/11. The ferry from the Statue of Liberty took us to Ellis Island, which is now a museum, but used to be the immigration station for all entering non-U.S. citizens.

It seems like we are gone a lot, but actually, we have a full slate of activities all the time here at home. With three live theaters, opera, concerts, square and round dancing, aerobics, Bible studies, church functions, library volunteer, Partners-in-Care driver, choir singing, all going on it's not easy to maintain our premises.

The following year, 2010, was a very eventful time, although we had only one out-of-the-country trip. The one trip in February was down the east coast of South America, which is quite different from the previous west coast trip. Even leaving was exciting. Maryland had record snowfall in early February. We had hardly dug out when another major snowfall was predicted to arrive Tuesday—the day we were to fly out of Dulles. Margaret attempted to move our flight to Monday or early Tuesday, but the airline said, "No space." They did say that Washington's Reagan had just opened for business after the last snowfall. We could fly if we could get there in an hour. Of course, that would be impossible. We knew that if we missed the ship, we couldn't catch up later as all the stops were tiny towns with no airport. To our delight our Oceania cruise line phoned and offered us early departure Tuesday. Great! Monday, we drove over Washington's beltway roads, which were still being plowed and were usually open on only one lane. We straggled into our hotel near Dulles airport, which offered to drive us to a restaurant in another hotel, because most of the roads were impassable. Great! The next morning we departed early from Dulles for Charlottesville and spent the day roaming up and down the airport waiting for our late evening flight. The morning flight out of Dulles left on time, but our previously scheduled afternoon flight was canceled as the next big snowstorm hit. Oceania's change saved our whole trip! The morning flight out of Dulles left on time, but our previously set afternoon flight was canceled as the next big snowstorm hit. Oceania's change saved our whole trip. There was no way that we could fly to an airport "en route" and catch up to the ship because all the ports were tiny villages long the coast of Brazil. From there the trip was a piece of cake. But everyone on the ship had a snow story to tell and the constant question was, "How did you get to the ship?"

Snow at home, Dec. 2009

Once we were aboard, we started in Brazil and cruised on down to Uruguay and Argentina. Our flight took us directly to Rio de Janeiro, where the ship Insignia of Oceania line was waiting. We got our room on board the first day and then had an all-day drip round the Rio area on the next day.

There was a very unusual cog railway ride through jungle flowers and up on a steep mountain called Hunchback. From the cog railway, we walked to an elevator up an even steeper climb and finally to an escalator that lifted us to the base of the famous statue. The statue of Christ of the Andes is 120 feet high. We walked all round the large plaza at the base of the statue viewing the city and harbor below. What a sight!

Christ above Buenos Aires, Brazil, on trip 2011

Our bus took us across town to the beaches where we saw hang gliders come down from an adjacent mountain. Rio is surrounded by high mountains. After a Brazilian lunch called Churrascaria, we went on two cable cars near the harbor and up Sugar Loaf Mountain. The first cable car went up Urca Hill to get close and then the second went to the top of Sugar Loaf, a 4290 foot one-piece granite rock sticking out of the water. Another spectacular sight of Rio! We returned down to the beach where I bought two huge cocoanuts that were punched open and we drank the juice with a straw.

At the next three ports in Brazil there were no special tours. The ship anchored off the shore of the towns and we took a ship's tender into the dock. The first town, Buzios, was 96 miles south of Rio. We simply walked around seeing the ships and tourist items. On the beach was a sand sculpture of a castle with large letters, "BUZIOS." Another spot had a sculpture of three bronze fishermen with their net.

The second anchorage was at Ilha Grande on down the coast from Rio. Many highly painted boats lined the dock, and their owners wished to hire out rides to tourists. The shops carried very bright clothes, table cloths, and towels. Another nights' cruise brought us down to Parati, Brazil, which was also an anchorage. We enjoyed the quaint architecture and walking round the town.

As usual, we cruised at night and spent the next day in port. This port was Santos, Brazil, where they had deep water so we could tie up at dock. In Santos, we boarded a tour bus for a ride to Sao Paulo, a much larger city over one hour away. Around this city, we enjoyed impressive buildings, including: The Cathedral, the Monastery, beautiful parks with gardens, public squares, the university with stadium, and a nice restaurant with Brazilian barbecue.

Brazil is a large country with a very long coastline, using up five nights of our trip, including part of each day at sea. Our final port in Brazil was Itajai, where we took another bus to nearby Camboriu City Resort. The highlight was the cable car rides. The first cable car was up to the Atlantic Forest Station, where we walked a forest trail with a local guide who described the flora and fauna. The next cable car went above the trees and down to Laranjeiras station, where we walked down to the beach and could have taken a dip. A final cable car carried us to Barra Sul Station, where we caught our bus back to the ship. These cable cars held us above the trees so we could see the jungle and flowers below.

We had a full day and night at sea before reaching Punta Del Este in Uruguay. There we traveled in a bus around town and down to beach resorts along the coast. Most unusual was a sculpture on the beach that consisted of 5 fingers of a hand sticking up out of the sand with only the last two joints showing. The parts showing were six to ten feet high. The illusion was of a buried hand. We also visited casa Pueblo, a most unusual white house with a museum owned by a famous local artist. The following day was in the capital of Uruguay, Montevideo. The term means "mountain view," and, while the city is on the water, the surrounding mountains are a view. We had a scenic bus drive around the old city with its parks and monuments.

Of particular note was the Legislative Palace, considered one of the three most beautiful legislative buildings in the world. We walked through and took many pictures, especially of the beautiful inlaid stone works. At Battle y Ordonez Park, we viewed and walked around the well-known ox cart monument. We also saw Prado Park and Independence Square. At Independence Square was the Gral Artigas monument commemorating the country's independence. On the way back to the ship in port, we drove past lovely homes in the residential areas. This was an extraordinarily picturesque city!

Our final stop on the cruise was Buenos Aires in Argentina, which is just across the bay from Montevideo. The ocean inlet separates the two countries. On the first of our three days in Argentina, we took a bus through the countryside to Tigre Delta on a large river. We traveled on Avenida del Libertador, passing through residential neighborhoods in Vincente Lopez, Martinez, Olivos, and San Isidoro. San Isidoro was impressive for its great cathedral, which we walked through. At Tigre Delta, we took a river boat with about 50 others for an hour scenic trip on the green labyrinth of channels and streams. Along the ride we passed villas, English gardens, rowing sculls, and natural uninhabited islands. That really showed off the lush coastal country.

The second day we toured more around the city of Buenos Aires. I particularly enjoyed the bright flowers in shops and the ceiling paintings in the mall. The third day was disembarkation day, but we still toured in the morning. Our bus took us to some outlandish neighborhoods where each house was painted in a collage of different bright colors, a weird area with weird ships. A most unusual sculpture dominated a park. It had huge, 50 foot high, steel petals in the shape of a tulip, that opened and closed during the day. At the city cemetery, I took a picture of the grave of the famous first lady, Evita Peron. Although she has been dead a number of years, local admirers still bring flowers to her grave.

Late in the day, we went to the airport and caught our plane all the way home from Buenos Aires.

As I mentioned, that year 2010, was full of unusual events. In January we had 24 inches of snow on the ground over several days. It is the most snow that we've had in 50 years, and required a private snow plow to clear our driveway. That snow was still on the ground when we left for the South American cruise in February. Later in February, we flew to Denver for our skiing with the Wolfes at Beaver Creek.

May that year was a dilly! We managed to attend 4 graduations of grandchildren. The first to graduate was Gary Behm from Messiah College in Pennsylvania. The next weekend we flew to Denver again for the graduation of Ryan Wolfe from his high school. The next weekend we flew back to Florida for the graduation of Jason Summers from his high school A little later, in Early June, we flew to Seattle, Washington for the graduation of Cara Wolfe from the University of Washington. It is notable that all four occurred on different weekends!

Just a month later was the tragedy of the year—the death of Ryan Wolfe right after his high school graduation. He had a heart failure that nobody could explain. The funeral was 10 July, 2010. The night that Ryan died in his sleep was the night before he and his father, Norman, were to fly east to visit and fish with me. So much for the temporal plans of man!

During all of this, we had construction going on for the new bath downstairs. It took almost 6 months. We held open house for our neighbors in January and, because of the snow, again in April. In July we hosted a block party for some 50 people, all to celebrate our new home.

Another major highlight was the wedding, August 22, in Pennsylvania. Grandson Brian Behm married Victoria in a formal ceremony at a fancy park resort not far from Philadelphia. The crying shame for me was that I couldn't attend, as I was in the hospital. On August 20, my doctor sent me in an ambulance from his office, where I had gone with symptoms of tiredness, to the hospital. My heartbeat was dangerously slow, down in the twenties instead of 70. The surgeon wanted to operate right away, but he was on duty in the emergency room. He postponed until the middle of the next day and then installed a pacemaker into my chest. That was August 21, the day before the wedding. Only the Lord kept me alive over the night and morning before the surgery. While the surgeon left it up to me, I didn't feel strong enough to attend the outdoor wedding. I did come home the next day on Monday, but was only home several days.

My arm and one foot swelled up huge, so I went to a clinic in town. That doctor called another ambulance to take me back to the hospital. Apparently I had a severe infection in my arm from the IV installed in the first ambulance. A dozen doctors came by my room that week and none could solve the problem of what I had! The end of the week they sent me back home again. Well, I was only home a night and a day. The following night, near midnight, I could not breathe enough oxygen and was suffocating. Margaret called the emergency number 911, and the third ambulance took me back to the hospital again.

This time the emergency room technician put me on pure oxygen overnight. The next morning the overnight attendant told me, "When you came in, I thought, 'This one will not make it till morning.'" Well, you need to see what the dear Lord, Christ, is doing before you draw conclusions! With pure oxygen I was still there in the morning, and went to another room. The doctor could see that my lungs were full of fluid and he put me on heavy diuretics. I was going every half hour for several days and nights. It was almost another week before I could go home again, still with a swollen arm and leg. All those doctors never found out what infection caused all the trouble. Note that the pacemaker worked fine and what almost killed me was the after infection! Life is an experience to cherish, to say the least.

In October that year, we spent our usual week in Ocean City on the beach. I went wading and flew my kite. Over the year we danced at three conventions in addition to our regular square and round dances at home. The conventions were in January, March, and July. Add to all these outside events our regular weekly activities at home.

What do you think? Do we need a break or vacation from the full schedule? Be it known: we are on vacation exactly 365 days every year!

CHAPTER 17

History Relived

I've always been interested in history and seeing where great events actually occurred. This year 2011, our overseas trip was to Russia with an Elderhostel program now called Road Scholar. They provide local scholars to give you the history and culture of what you are seeing. It means so much more to know what it is and how it got there than to just admire the beauty.

Our overseas flight in August took us directly to Moscow, the capitol, where we checked into the Cosmos Hotel. It is a large modern hotel built inn an arc shape. Interesting is the statue of French leader De Gaulle, prominently displayed in front of the arc. I understand the French government donated money to build the hotel for the Moscow Olympics. I think they had a French architect too. Through our room window we could see memorials to the Soviet space flight, including a space ship and a high needle spire.

The next day, a bus took our group to Red Square, the center of Russian rule for many centuries. We walked by Lenin's Mausoleum—at a good distance because it was behind a fence and visited only by standing in a long line. We also went by the Kremlin clock tower, and viewed the architectural grandeur of famous St. Basil's cathedral. St. Basil, built in the 16th century, commemorates the Russian victory over the Tartars and is thought to contain the Russian soul. Its onion shaped and highly colored spires give the cathedral extraordinary beauty!

Moscow, Russia trip, 2011, St. Basil

Across the huge Red Square from St. Basil's, we noted the long lines, at least a half mile, of people trying to get into the building to view Lenin's tomb. I don't think it was worth the long wait. However, we did go into the Armory Chamber where the cultural treasures of Russia are on display. The Russian czars' royal jewels, crowns with 10,000 diamonds, and the most elaborate robes are on view. Also, the all-gold covered horse drawn carriages were there and ready to go. They highlighted famous Faberge eggs and a large collection of medieval arms. This was another world wonder to see and experience!

That evening we checked into our boat or river cruiser on the Moscow River. The cruiser holds over a hundred passengers along with our group of 30 some elderhostelers, plus some twenty crew members. The next day was back in Moscow to visit the Kremlin Palace, more cathedrals, many government buildings, and the legendary Tsar Cannon also with the Tsar Bell. I have my picture next to that great cannon, the largest cannon in the world. It has never been fired—it's just for display now as is the great bell. They proved that they could cast such monsters! The bell was so large that the tower supports broke, bringing the bell down and cracking it. It reminds us of the Liberty Bell.

Of particular interest was the Cathedral of Ascension, which was outside the office of Joseph Stalin in the Kremlin. The church bells, dating from 1172, were so annoying to Stalin that he had the entire cathedral blown up, leaving a nasty hole in the ground next to the Moscow River. In order to fill the hole, a later leader had a swimming pool installed. Our tour guide said she herself had swum in that pool. Finally, in 1992, Boris Yeltsin gave the land back to the Russian Orthodox Church so that the cathedral—which had been like St. Peter's is to the Roman Catholic Church—could be rebuilt. From pictures and old plans the cathedral was reconstructed to the exact image of the original 12th century building. The original took 44 years to build, but the reconstruction took only 7 years. The common citizens donated the money for that reconstruction. Say something for us common people everywhere!

After a night in the docked ship, we had an extensive bus tour of the rest of Moscow. Along the way we viewed the Moscow University, a convent, many squares, and the cathedral of Christ the Savior. Near the University still stood the ski jump from the Winter Olympics of many years ago. In a park on the edge of the convent was a statue of a bronze duck followed by eight little ducklings. The statues were donated to Moscow by the US president's wife, Barbara Bush, when she was there for a state visit. She wanted something for the Russian children. However, the tourists were all taking turns sitting on the largest duck. The convent is again in operation, but no longer has that parkland as part of its holdings. In general the architecture and beauty of the important buildings was top notch.

We set sail at dinner that evening and began our multi-day journey to St. Petersburg. We began navigating the Moscow River, took locks to a canal to a large lake, and then locks to the Neva River at St. Petersburg. Actually there were 17 locks along the way, each of which raised or lowered the ship about 50 feet. Most of these locks were met in the night hours because we stayed in ports during the day. The oldest locks, near St. Petersburg, were built by Peter the Great to launch his ocean going ships. Well, he designed the locks and ordered their construction. His serfs built the canals and locks at a great loss of life. Stalin ordered the construction of the canals and locks from the Moscow River to the lake. He used prisoners for the labor—again at a great loss of life.

During the first full day's sailing, we had extensive lectures on Russian history, going back to the ninth century. The country passed back and forth between the Vikings, the Swedes, the Arabs, and whoever was raiding through the land. It's a very long story. Of interest was the development of Moscow. The local tribal leader, probably the same one who put up the first Kremlin Walls, was successful in conquering the other tribes in the neighboring territories.

The first tour on our voyage was Ouglich. We had walking excursions of the two main cathedrals, one of St. Dmitry and the other the Transfiguration Cathedral. Tsarevich Dmitry was mysteriously killed here in 1591, so the building is known as the church of spilled blood. The palace of Dmitry has been moved to the Kremlin fortress.

The next town, the next day, was supposed to be Yaroslavl, but because of dense fog, we stopped at Rylinsk instead. The name Rylinsk means "fish town" because the major industry used to be supplying sturgeon fish to the area. These fish were eliminated when the locks were installed because the fish couldn't swim upriver to spawn. There was a statue to the "boat haulers" who pulled the barges along the river with ropes—not donkeys or horses—people! The haulers walked in bare feet and had a life span of 35 years! Has civilization made some progress?

A main street in Rylinsk was called "standing street," named in the 17th century because that is where the locals in the labor force stood until hired. The museum in town featured the chair given to Empress Catherine the Great when she visited. Catherine returned the chair for them to remember her. During Stalin's time, the local church was used for grain storage! It had been returned later to the Russian Orthodox Church. While we were there a church service was going on, so we sneaked in to watch. No one sat—no chairs. A big casket was carried in, so it was some funeral service. We found out that they were commemorating the Chernobyl atomic disaster.

The guide, who spoke only Russian, pointed out a local distinction—a statue of Lenin standing. She said it is the only statue of Lenin depicting him with his hand thrust into his coat-like Napoleon. She also said, the town wanted to remove the statue and replace it with the statue which used to be there—one of Czar Alexander, but that statue had been lost and hadn't been found yet.

We loved seeing a town that was "real." Women were selling their farm produce from small baskets on the street. Small shops were open. The streetcars were operating in the street. No one was selling tourist trinkets!

The next town we visited was Goritzy on the Volga River, near the northern edge of old Russia. We walked through their old monastery that was built as a fortress. In "the time of the troubles," the Poles attacked this fortress and held a siege for 6 years, but never brought it down. In its heyday, there were 600 monks in residence, and Czar Michael, the first Romanov, gave the monastery an elaborate gate. When Peter the Great came along, he confiscated the bells to melt them into cannon. By the time of Stalin, the monastery was down to 5 monks and was turned into a museum. Is that progress?

Our cruise continued north across Lake Onega, second largest lake in Europe, to the island of Kizhi, a UNESCO listed site. Here we marveled at the Cathedral of the Transfiguration, a spectacular wooden construction with 22 onion domes, all fashioned from bark and local trees. The cathedral was built in 1714, the pieces perfectly fit together without a single nail! Do we have any work that accurate today? Those 22 domes were carved out of ash wood by hand by one man. The sides of the cathedral are of a very hard pine tree. This large church is only used in the summer. A quite small church down the path is used during the winter.

Only a handful of folks live on the island, and their main occupation is teaching schoolchildren and tourists about early Russian agriculture.

Interesting is the life style of the local inhabitants. To emulate their ancestors, they raise and flay their own wheat, care for the horses and cattle, and grow their other food. In the past, because there is not enough grazing land on the island, the islanders would put one cow at a time in a small boat and row it over to another island to feed. This process continued until the entire herd was on the fresh island. The women rowed across to the other island twice a day to milk the cows. The cows learned easily to tolerate the boat ride since they discovered that each boat ride meant a new island with fresh grass. The women also did their own spinning without a spinning wheel. Try to figure that!

On the island was a windmill, dating from the time of Peter the Great, 1696-1725. He had seen them in Holland and brought the idea to Russia. This windmill was on a rotating base so it could always face the wind. It was used to grind the wheat kernels. The island Russian Orthodox priest was also curator of the museum because he had such a small congregation. One small wooden church on the island was 600 years old, still standing and still useable.

Our final stop before Saint Petersburg was at Mandrogy on the Svir River. On the river shore was a reproduction of a typical rural Russian settlement, a feature for tourists. It was called a "green stop" because it so well fit the environment. We had lunch on shore consisting of "Shish Kabob."

Our last day of sailing was across the largest lake in Europe, called Lake Ladoga. This lake is larger than all of our Great Lakes. It was strategic in WWII because, frozen, it provided a passage for goods into besieged St. Petersburg, and an escape route for fugitives. From the lake, we cruised the Neva River that flows through St. Petersburg. The dock was at the near side of St. Petersburg. We slept on the boat during the three days stay.

The morning we docked was immediately followed by a bus tour of the city and in particular the Saint Peter and St. Paul fortress. Our lectures were on the history and architecture of St. Petersburg, both very fascinating. The town was laid out by Peter I, called Peter the Great, in a well-planned grid in 1703. The nobles all were required to build fine palaces along the Neva River. Peter stayed in the elaborate fortress on the island guarding the harbor. The cathedral in the fortress, considered the birthplace of the city, contained the burial caskets of all the Romanov Tsars. We had a packed lunch box so we could eat in a park and continue viewing.

The afternoon was spent in the world famous Hermitage Museum, built by Catherine the Great. She called it a Hermitage because she alone visited it. It was her private retreat. It houses an extensive art collection representing all eras. They had paintings of the old masters, Italian, Dutch, Spanish, and French. One portrait gallery was of the 1812 siege of the city by the French. While the French got pieces, they never took over the whole city because resistance was so fierce. In particular we went in the throne room and some ballrooms, all spectacularly decorated. After dinner on the boat, we took in a National Dance and Music performance that featured Russian music.

The next day, talks were on the Romanov dynasty, and our bus went to the town of Pushkin, site of the summer residences of the Tsars. In particular, we went through the fabulous palace of Catherine the Great, who ruled from 1762 to 1796. She expanded the palace from 100 rooms to 300 rooms. The rooms and great hall are decorated in the baroque style, the very last word in elaborate art. In particular the Amber Room is completely covered with palm-sized pieces of amber—all the walls. I have a booklet of palace pictures and a separate booklet on just the amber room. This is in addition to my personal pictures. Catherine had in her palace 1500 dresses. How does that compare with the one dress of most peasant women?

The building was occupied by the Nazis in World War II, and completely burned. It is now restored to its original state and all the amber has been replaced. Similarly beautiful are the gardens, lake, and surrounding separate buildings, such as the Turkish bath. Catherine considered herself especially beautiful and showed off her shoulders in low dresses. How up to date would she be today?

We were wondering how a cash-strapped Russia (and Soviet Union) could spend so much money to restore these excessively grand buildings. We were told that the government thought it was important to show how lavishly the aristocrats lived so that succeeding generations would understand why a revolution was necessary. Indeed, as one views all this extravagance, one wonders why anyone thought he needed to live like this. Or how one person could amass so much wealth.

That evening we went to the Aurora Palace Theatre to see the famous Russian Ballet dance Swan Lake. They dance like no other ballet in the world and are the very best!

Our final full day was spent in Peterhof, the stunning summer residence of Peter the Great, right on the Baltic Sea. It is just a few miles north of St. Petersburg. St. Petersburg was the crowning achievement of Peter, a conquered territory and designed city which allowed Russia to gain access to shipping on the Baltic. Prior to Peter, Russia had no access to European culture and economy. Soon after conquering this land, Peter moved his capitol to St. Petersburg, and spent time on these waters in his own sailboat. We didn't see the interior of the palace on this trip, apparently because it is very similar to Catherine's palace. However vast grounds surround the buildings. Peter the Great took his inspiration from Versailles and intended to impress foreign visitors. Most impressive to me were the hundreds of fountains over the park and down to the Grand Cascade. A whole river is brought down from a neighboring mountain to feed these many fountains with very high jets of water. All the connections are from underground out-of-sight pipes. At the bottom of the sloping gardens is the Grand Cascade with dozens of gold covered statues all spouting water, the central stream going all the way as high as the five story palace in the background. Don't shortchange Russian engineering and architecture!

On the way back, we again toured the city, St. Petersburg, with the University museum, and many more palaces. Similar to Venice, Italy, the city is laid out on a grid of rivers and canals. Each palace faces the water. This city is the fantasy of Peter, along with his nobles who were reluctant, but required to build palaces in the city.

You may remember that after the Russian Revolution of 1917, the City was named Petrograd, "City of Peter" because a "burg" sounded German. Later it was renamed Leningrad—"City of Lenin" to eliminate religious references and honor the Soviet Leader. Recently the town people voted to return to the original name of St. Petersburg, Lenin being somewhat discredited. However, the outlying county/district decided to retain Lenin as their name. The older folks liked the socialist protections, which have been lost in the competitive capitalist state.

The rest of the year 2011, was filled with many other activities, not as dramatic as in Russia. In February we skied with the Colorado Wolfes and the Behms at our favorite Beaver Creek in the Rockies. March saw us back in the Caribbean on a new Oceania ship called Marina. The new ship was the height of luxury with top notch meals all 12 days. It was just commissioned the previous year.

The marina went to a number of islands new to us. In the British Virgin Islands, we visited Tortola and St. Barth, where we saw the town of Gustavia, enjoying all the jungle greenery and flowers. On Dominica, we were in Roseau and also saw the countryside. On island St. Lucia, we docked at Soufriere, a French town. This island was quite different. Besides the Diamond Botanical Gardens, it had spectacular waterfalls and volcanic mineral baths. The volcanic basin was covered with hot steaming bubbling pools. I have many spectacular pictures of the steam and the rugged land. From there, we cruised on to St. Johns on Antigua and the island Virgin Gorda. On the way home we stopped at the far eastern end of the Dominican Republic, where we saw ancient caves with wall paintings over a thousand years old. People always seem to try to leave a message for future generations. Our final stop was on Grand Turk Island before returning to Miami. That was a most pleasant cruise out of the winter cold!

That May, the Summers family came North to our home. Kevin brought his girl friend, Alise, whom he married a year later. We all had a fine time boating, fishing, and enjoying the water.

Late summer in September was Gary Behm's wedding. The wedding rehearsal, followed by dinner, was right here at my house on South River.

I have pictures of the couple under my "bridal arch," leading to the beach. It was a great occasion and location. The wedding itself was held on Sunday, the next day, at the Mayo Beach Park, near the end of our Mayo Peninsula. At the mouth of South River, it has a fine view across the Chesapeake Bay. Everything went beautifully.

Our last trip that year was to our usual condo in Ocean City, right on the Atlantic Ocean beach. Our week is the first part of October and the weather was just ideal. I get to fly my kites on the beach and walk out into the water. As usual, we bought a hand painted picture, actually two this time, for our new house. The pictures are hung in the game room downstairs. I really like the water scenes and bright colors.

CHAPTER 18

NOW

I've read that the most important word in the English language is "NOW." Now is the time for salvation. Now is the time for evangelization. Now is the time to pull your life together and get moving. Now is the time to speak out and encourage and help build the Kingdom of God!

Have you been thinking of starting something good? Maybe a Bible study, maybe an exercise program, maybe a help or food program for the needy. Now is the time to commence!

In this ongoing biography, I am up to the year 2012. Guess what year this is on the calendar? Yes, 2012—it is now!

In February, we exited the cold up here in Maryland, and we sopped up the warmth down in the Caribbean on another cruise. This was the first of 3 cruises this year and we went to some new locations for us. The winter cruise on the Oceania ship Marina started in Miami and went first to Key West, Florida. We toured the interesting sights including a large marker for "the southernmost point in U.S." There were ports of call along the Central American coast, including Mexico, Honduras, Guatemala, Belize, and then back to islands Cozumel and Cayman. It's all an adventure with swimming, snorkeling, and experiencing the jungle Flora.

At Roatan, we marveled over the tropical Gumbalimba Park. In Guatemala, we rode a small river boat inland to on old Spanish Fort, built in 1595. On Cozumel, we bussed the entire coastline seeing elaborately costumed Spanish dancers at one ranch and the Cristino Gardens at another stop. There is no end to the new sights and new places!

The second cruise was over my 85th birthday, 11 June 2012. We had a most memorable birthday party with the entire Wolfe family, 23 persons in all. Our guests were our children, grandchildren, cousins, and all their spouses. The guest list included children: Cynthia and Greg Behm; Eileen and Jim Summers; Norman and Nancy Wolfe; grandchildren: David Behm and fiancé Tirza Ridgely; Brian and Victoria Behm; Gary and Claire Behm; Cara Wolfe and brother Mark Wolfe; Kevin and Alise Summers; Jason Summers and sister Karen Summers; cousin Kay Barrans and her niece, Rachel Wolfe and her granddaughter, Jennifer Fair.

Brian Behm designed a special logo which Margaret had screen printed on white and blue caps, one a gift for each participant. I still wear my hat frequently. The children each contributed photos from our and their lives together. Cynthia Behm collected them all, collated them, and created a lovely book displaying the photos. The book was their gift to Margaret and me. It is fun to review all those photos reminding us of times spent together over fifty years.

My actual birthday date sparked a very lively party at the dinner tables with cake, trimmings, and me dancing with a waiter. Anything can happen.

Margaret & Eileen, 2012

Norman & Cynthia, 2012

For that trip, we chose the Carnival line because we had so many young people along. They all had a ball and did their own thing in the ports while all of us ate together in the evening main dining room. The ship revisited, for Margaret and me, the ports of Cozumel, Belize, Mahogany Bay on Roatan, and Grand Cayman. We took different tours from the ones on the previous ship.

Our overseas trip this year was a cruise on the Danube River in September—October. It was partly celebrating Margaret's birthday, number 80, on September 29. We toured the Eastern Bloc countries of Romania, Bulgaria, Serbia, Croatia, and Hungary. This tour was with Viking Cruises who provided guides and lecturers along the way for all of the local color.

Our flight from Newark, NJ, was directly to Bucharest, Romania., the capitol city. We had a very nice hotel the two days in Bucharest, founded in the 14th century and chosen capitol in 1859 with the merger of Moldavia and Walachia. Bucharest is remarkable in beauty and architecture. Their parliament building, called "House of the People," is the largest in all Europe and second in size to only our Pentagon. However, the architecture of our Pentagon doesn't hold a candle to that of "House of the People." Both inside and outside are great pieces of art, the elaborate columns, decorated arches, and outstanding paintings on all walls and ceilings. Circular marble staircases go up a half dozen stories to innumerable banquet and meeting rooms. The big halls are about the size of a football field!

Other great sights in Bucharest are Victory Square, the National Theatre, the 17th century Patriarchal church, and a large central park. In this park is a completely reconstructed authentic Romanian village from out in the countryside with its rural cottages, farmhouses, stalls, horse carriages, and water mills. We got to see all that right there without traveling outside the capitol.

In the afternoon, our bus drove to the port city of Giurgiu on the Danube River, where we found our stateroom on the cruise ship for the next week. Giurgiu is close to the mouth of the Danube at the Black Sea. That first night, the ship merely crossed the river to Ruse, Bulgaria. Note that the Danube is the border between the countries Romania and Bulgaria. Early morning another bus took us on an all day tour inside Bulgaria. The bus took us to Arbanasi, a lovely village where we saw the frescoes in the Nativity Church and had lunch with native costumed dancers. The afternoon was mainly in the former Bulgarian capital of Veliko Tarnovo with a walk up Tsaravets Hill with its view of the royal castle ruins. We walked another street of quaint shops of local handicrafts and native clothing all in the ancient architecture. So impressive!

In the evening we rejoined our ship for dinner at its dock in Svistov, Bulgaria, a ways upriver from Ruse where the ship had let us off. After dinner, aboard we always had entertainment—music, dancing or both. Our river cruise ship was a catamaran, two hulls, and about 200 feet long with close to 200 passengers on 3 decks.

The next day our motor coach drove us from Vidin on to Belogradshick, still in Bulgaria. There we walked through the many terraced courtyards of the Belogradshick Fortress, that was last used during the time of the Serbian-Bulgarian War of 1885. From the Fortress you could view the very irregular red rock formations towering up from the nearby hills. Those high weathered formations resembled silhouettes of people, animals, ships, palaces and mushrooms. The scene reminded me of the bright red rocks in Utah and northern Arizona. What a spectacular sight! Back in Vidin on our agenda was the Baba Vida fortress that was built over hundreds of years from the 10th to the 13th centuries. In town the churches covered the principal religions, the Orthodox Church, the Osman Mosque, and the Jewish synagogue.

The next morning after a long overnight cruise, we docked back on the Romania side in Orsova. We simply walked through town to view the Cathedral with its very unusual curved roof, a masterpiece of engineering. The highlight of this day was our cruise through the "Iron Gate," an extremely dangerous narrow, fast water gorge with high white limestone cliffs. Today dams have slowed the water so ships can navigate. Previously many ships were lost or destroyed trying to navigate the rapids. Our ship had two powerful motors to maintain speed against the current.

I particularly enjoyed the great bearded face covering one cliff. A wealthy man spent a million dollars hiring some 40 carvers for 10 years to cut out the great face. Actually, it is similar to the presidents' faces on Mount Rushmore in South Dakota. Various caves along the river edge provided shelter and a hiding place during historic sieges over the ages back to Roman times. Now most of them are filled with water because of the dams.

In the morning, we woke up in the capitol city Belgrade, Serbia. Note the country used to be called Yugoslavia, until the breakup with Croatia. Of interest was the story of our lead guide aboard ship. She was a young woman in her late 20's and lived near Belgrade. While living in the same house, she was a citizen over time of 4 different countries! How do you like that for national stability! How we need to thank God for our home, our country, and so many blessings.

Belgrade, meaning "white fortress," is at the confluence of the Danube and Sava Rivers. We walked through the Fortress, now a park that overlooks the two rivers. It's a breathtaking scene through medieval gates and down to the water. You can't just read, you have to get up and go!

After breakfast and a morning ride up the river, we arrived at Vukovar, Croatia, on the south and west side of the Danube. Croatia is on both sides of the Danube, as is Hungary. Vukovar, near the junction of the Drava and Danube rivers was a strategic location during the Croatian-Serbian War in the early 1990's. Another bus took us a few miles to Osijek, the fourth largest city in Croatia. We still saw a lot of debris around from the war-destroyed buildings. The story is that, of some 25,000 men holding the town during the war siege, 21,000 were killed. It's very hard to comprehend the carnage and destruction. My thoughts go back to our Civil War in the 1860's. Anyway, we took note of the beautiful Baroque architecture that remained and the neo-Gothic Church of St. Peter and St. Paul. The country of Croatia, as well as Serbia, reaches all the way down to the Adriatic Sea on the Mediterranean.

Another day, another port. This time it was Kalocsa, Hungary. The Danube had turned north and Kalocsa was on the east side. In town we visited the Archbishop's Palace, and then a long bus ride took us to the interior country for the Bakodpuszta Equestrian Center. The Center is on a large flat plain and has stands like a stadium on one side. We sat on benches for the show, along with several hundred other visitors. First by was a large wagon pulled by four horses, guided by the driver. Four horses are tough to handle. Then the individual horsemen, that I believe are called Cossacks, rode across the field at high speed. Each one had a large whip, which he cracked repeatedly in the air on the dash by. They were in elaborate Cossack dress and were very colorful. Next, they set up foot-high columns with a rectangular 6-inch block on top. The idea was to knock the block off with a crack of the whip as the horse and rider dashed by. There were 4 such set-ups, maybe 20 yards apart, across a parallel in front of the stands. At least 10 riders rode by at top speed, twirling their whips overhead and cracking at each block. Most of them actually hit 3 of the 4 blocks. However, there were two horsemen who knocked all four blocks off the columns. It was a dramatic spectacle!

The finale was a bareback rider standing astride two horses with four horses in a row in front of them and two more horses in front of the four, guiding all eight horses with eight reins in his hands. He circled the entire field and brought the eight horses up before the viewers. Let's see you try it! That night aboard ship was the Captain's Farewell Dinner, a real feast.

In the morning, we docked in Budapest, Hungary, the Hungarian capitol, a large city that has about 1/3 of the entire population of Hungary. Note that Buda is the city on the west bank and Pest is the city on the East bank of the Danube. When they combined with bridges to form the Capitol, obviously Budapest. After checking out of the ship we rode a nice motor coach around Pest while our luggage was delivered directly to our hotel in Buda. Pest is the more modern side, and the flat side, containing the Parliament house, the National Opera House and Heroes' Square along with most businesses. Heroes Square is huge, like the mall in Washington, with innumerable statues of local leaders back a thousand years. We used two of the many bridges across the Danube in going back and forth.

The Buda side is very steep and our hotel was at the top of one mountain. Just outside the hotel were defensive towers and a walk from which you could look 'way down to the river and bridges below. Our walk around the top included seeing the castle complex, the Bastion, and a large military museum with statues outside of men wearing all the many different military uniforms over the ages. The ultra-modern hotel had an excavated side, which contained ancient stone walls. The hotel had set it out as a trendy grotto bar. The views along the walkway are just marvelous and I took many pictures.

For entertainment, we took in two shows on our own. The first night we saw the circus in Pest. It included all the usual acrobatics, high wire acts, and clowns. You didn't need to know the language to enjoy it. After finding out how unreasonably high the cab fare was that night, we took a local city bus the second night to an operetta in Pest. The only negative was that we got lost trying to find the Operetta House. It was a couple of blocks away from the Opera House. Fortunately we found the concierge of an establishment who spoke enough English to direct us. The show had subtitles in English above the stage so we could follow the story, which was sung in Hungarian. The plot was very racial with the heroine first being thought to be Jewish (she was an orphan), bad enough, although the local Ghetto took her in, and then being proven to have had Lutheran parents—the very rock bottom. Remember the Hungarians are all orthodox and the Lutherans are considered to be villains. Needless to say, that play would not go over in the U.S. We just say, "What's the big deal?"

Except for breakfast in the hotel, we ate locally on our own the two days in Budapest. Of course, the final day they took us to the airport for our flight back to Newark, NJ. Since we arrived very late in the US, we stayed in a hotel in Newark overnight and flew home the next day. As you can see, this was a major addition to our world travels!

The three cruises were not the whole year. We enjoyed our other activities along with two family weddings. Kevin Summer, Eileen's oldest son, married Alise Gore in May of 1012. Of course we went to Florida for the lovely wedding and participated in a big wedding dinner with all the guests. That was the first wedding in the Summer family. Eileen and Jim's other two children, Jason and Karen, are now in college.

Then, in September of 2012, we flew to Colorado for the wedding of David Behm to Tirza Ridgely. This was another formal wedding in a beautiful setting with a large crowd of guests. We were in the foothills with a great view of mountains all around. David was the third wedding of a child for Cynthia and Greg, as now all three of their sons are married and very happy.

In January of 2012 we flew to Colorado for skiing at Beaver Creek. I skied with my son, Norman, who is very patient with me on the easy slopes. On his own, Norman does all the roughest double black diamond slopes, very steep.

Margaret and I danced at our usual out of town conventions in March and July, along with our regular club dances each month. A new experience was the extreme weather at home. The very end of June, we had what they call a "derecho." I call it a tornado, extremely unusual here in Maryland. The wind took down five trees near our property, three of them huge—over 100-foot tall trees. One big tree hit our garage, caving the roof in along with some side and back walls. Amazingly, and a blessing, was that neither car inside the garage was touched.

The largest tree, a 120-foot oak, landed in our front yard with a huge limb crashing into the front corner of our house. It took out two walls and four windows. The total damage came to $50,000—completely covered by our house insurance. Finally, the third big tree came down on our back upper deck, crashing into the wooden railing and one supporting post. The screens were knocked out on the porch deck below. Since the trees took out the street electric lines, here and elsewhere, our power was off for 6 days. We camped out with the Behms because the heat was unbearable in the house. Our good neighbor with a generator hooked up our refrigerators so our food didn't spoil. Our house was the worst hit in our neighborhood and all the neighbors drove their cars by to gawk at the branches obscuring the house. The event was some shock to us, but all is now repaired.

As if that damage was not more than enough, the following October, another severe wind brought a neighbor's big tree down on the other side of our garage—the street side. It took the roof and back wall out, but another blessing, neither car inside was touched. This damage required another $25,000 to redo the street side and roof. Again insurance covered the damage and repairs have been completed. We have lived in Loch Haven for 54 years and this year was the only one in which we have sustained notable damage!

Two cousins, Cindy Murphy and Jonathan Stewart, visited this fall to do research on the Stewart family back to colonial times. Stewart was my mother's maiden name. We keep a genealogy record of these Stewarts and also of the Wolfes.

Finally, we hosted Julie Campbell, our church sponsored missionary to Kenya, Africa, on two occasions this fall. Margaret's letters keep family members abreast of our usual activities, including the New York trip in December to see the New York City Radio Center Christmas spectacular.

Well, this is it. After many years of writing, I'm up to the end of 2012, up to "NOW." My wish for you is the blessing of walking daily with the Holy Spirit, building the Kingdom of God, enjoying a life of peace, happiness, and fulfillment.

Carvel S. Wolfe
Dec. 2012